Discerning The Kingdom Of God

By Paul David Harrison
and Joy Burns Harrison

Published by
Messengers of His Kingdom
P.O. Box 833351
Richardson, TX 75080
Website: www.messengersofhiskingdom.com

First printing, August 2005
Second printing, December 2005
Third printing, October 2007

ISBN #1-932710-39-6

Pneumatikos Publishing
P.O. 595351
Dallas, TX 75359
www.pneumatikos.com or
Info@pneumatikos.com

Cover Art Work by Fabian Arroyo

Unless otherwise noted, scripture quotations are from the
HOLY BIBLE, Authorized King James Version.

Table of Contents

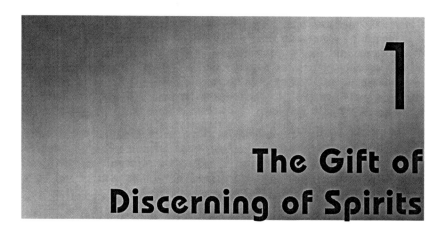

The Gift of Discerning of Spirits

Introduction

The mightiest days of the church are upon us. The Lord is calling for His saints to partner with His angels to arise and take dominion of this earth. The heavens are being opened as we intercede on the Father's behalf. The very land that we stand on is crying out for the sons of God to rise up and take this planet.

For the earnest expectation of the creature waiteth for the manifestation of the sons of God.

—ROMANS 8:19

For we know that the whole creation groaneth and travaileth in pain together until now.

—ROMANS 8:22

However, just like in a chess game, our opponent has made some counter moves to try and stop the things the Lord is doing. The activity of the spirit realm has increased exponentially as all the players get ready for the Lord's final moves. Saints are being summoned by the Lord to stand against the onslaught of the enemy. Graciously, God is preparing His children to be able to know how to stand against the wiles of the enemy. The warfare tactics of the past will not be sufficient for what we are going to be facing in the spirit realm.

As the Lord opens our spiritual eyes to the realms of the spirit, it is becoming more and more difficult to distinguish between what is of the Lord and what is of the enemy. The Word tells us the enemy transforms himself into an angel of light. One of the main reasons the enemy transforms himself is so he can infiltrate the house of the Lord and create various kinds of deceptions. Hence the warning of Jesus in Matthew 24, *"be not deceived,"* rings in our ears.

The purpose of this book is to relate the absolute necessity of receiving the gift of discerning of spirits and learning how to function in this gift on an ongoing basis. In addition, we would like to share personally how this gift has transformed our ability to enter and walk in the Kingdom of God.

Before we begin, it is necessary to distinguish between perceiving things of the spirit realm and discernment. We will discuss spiritual perceptions such as seeing and hearing in the spirit realm, but that is not discernment. Discernment does rely on our spiritual senses and our senses must be exercised and used. However, just perceiving something in the spirit realm is not discernment.

But strong meat belongeth to them that are of full age, even those who by reason of use have their senses exercised to **discern** *both good and evil.*

—HEBREWS 5:14

Scripture says discernment is the ability to know the things of God, to know what is good and what is evil. Through the promptings of the Holy Spirit you are able to tell the difference between the righteous and wicked, the profane and the holy, the clean and the unclean. You know what is of the Kingdom of God and what is not.

But the natural man receiveth not the things of the Spirit of God: for they are foolishness unto him: neither can he know them, because they are spiritually **discerned.**

—1 CORINTHIANS 2:14

And they shall teach my people the difference between the holy and profane, and cause them to **discern** *between the unclean and the clean.*
— EZEKIEL 44:23

. . . **discern** *good and bad. . .*
—2 SAMUEL 14:17, 1 KINGS 3:9

*. . .I **discern** between good and evil. . .*
                                    —*2 SAMUEL 19:35*

*. . .**discern** between the righteous and the wicked, between him that serveth God and him that serveth him not.*
                                    —*MALACHI 3:18*

Discernment goes even farther, it knows the timing of God and the judgment of God in a given situation. Discernment knows the thoughts, intents and understandings of individuals only as they are revealed by God and His Word. Discernment knows what is of the soul and what is of the spirit.

*Whoso keepeth the commandment shall feel no evil thing: and a wise man's heart **discerneth** both time and judgment.*
                                    —*ECCLESIATES 8:5*

*. . . understanding to **discern** judgment;*
                                    —*1 KINGS 3:11*

*. . . **discern** the signs of the times?*
                                    —*MATTHEW 16:3, LUKE 12:56*

*And beheld among the simple ones, I **discerned** among the youths, a young man void of understanding,*
                                    —*PROVERBS 7:7*

*For the word of God is quick, and powerful, and sharper than any twoedged sword, piercing even to the dividing asunder of soul and spirit, and of the joints and marrow, and is a **discerner** of the thoughts and intents of the heart.*
                                    —*HEBREWS 4:12*

Two Powerful Gifts

One day during prayer, I had a conversation with the Lord. He reminded me "Paul, think about the two very special gifts the Holy Spirit has given to your church. Think about how they have revolutionized your walk with Me." Any of you who have visited The Father's Church in Dallas, Texas, know that we preach, teach and practice the gift of divers tongues. Anytime the Lord releases a team to go out from our church, the primary message released is divers tongues. One of the major things that the gift of divers tongues does for the believer is empower him to become a mighty intercessor. Everything that we accomplish for the Lord begins with a voice, an intercessor's voice. **So the first gift we want to mention is the gift of divers tongues.** (1 Corinthians 12:10)

> *And the angel took the censer, and filled it with fire of the altar, and cast it into the earth: and there were **voices**, and thunderings, and lightnings, and an earthquake.*
>
> *—REVELATION 8:5*

For an individual or church to fully enter into partnering with the Lord for taking dominion of this planet, they will have to commit their life to intercession. To discern the realms discussed in this book takes dedication. This is not just a simple case of laying on of hands and receiving an impartation. It is not that easy, nor is it God's way. God's way is through establishing a relationship with His people. It is through intercession that we become the friends of God. Scripture says that God tells His friends what He is doing. It takes time to be a friend of God.

> *Surely the Lord GOD will do nothing, but <u>he revealeth his secret unto his servants the prophets.</u>* *—AMOS 3:7*

> <u>*Henceforth I call you not servants;*</u> *for the servant knoweth not what his lord doeth: <u>but I have called you friends; for all things that I have heard of my Father I have made known unto you.</u>* *—JOHN 15:15*

The second gift is the gift of discerning of spirits. It was through this powerful gift that God allowed us to experience His Kingdom in ways we once thought impossible. Unfortunately, these two gifts are often overlooked for the more prominent and visible gifts like, words of wisdom and knowledge, healing and miracles, and prophecy. Instead of being viewed as essential gifts, divers tongues and discerning of spirits are more often looked upon as less significant. To learn more about divers tongues, we highly recommend Pastor Ron Crawford's book, *Divers Tongues.* The book you are now reading, as its title suggests, is about the gift of discerning of spirits.

Make no mistake; Jesus knew exactly how critical the gift of discerning of spirits would be for the end-time believer. In fact, in one of Jesus' final declarations to His disciples, He warns them regarding the deceptive spiritual atmosphere that would encompass the earth in the last days. In Matthew 24, Jesus describes in numerous ways how

4

deceptions would come. He used phrases and terms like, "be not deceived", "believe it not", "false Christs", "false prophets" and "watch therefore".

It is imperative that we establish a biblical foundation for the importance of being able to operate in this gift. We truly believe the admonishment Jesus gave His disciples concerning the final days, and know it is essential that we welcome this magnificent gift into our life. We must be trained in the practicality of using it as we walk with the Lord. Our desire is to help you learn how to utilize this gift in intercession and in your daily life.

The Lord is welcoming the corporate body of Christ to experience His Kingdom in an unprecedented way. It should not come as a surprise to us that His Kingdom is being revealed. Jesus taught His disciples to pray, *"Thy kingdom come."*

In these last days, His Kingdom is coming, the heavens are opening, and the realms of the spirit are being made available for God's people to enter. Please understand that there are no shortcuts to accessing the doors into which the Father wants to lead you. The great danger in taking shortcuts is the potential for accidentally succumbing to a deception. The spirit realm is full of doorways, gates and access points. As we come to know the Lord in an intimate way, He teaches us which doors access Him and which ones would lead to alternate paths.

> *Because strait is the gate, and narrow is the way, which leadeth unto life, and few there be that find it.*
> *—MATTHEW 7:14*

Those who have committed to interceding and partnering for the will of God to be done on earth are able to access the hidden places in Christ. Scripture says the saints will partner with God to possess the Kingdom. It is our commitment to the "thy will be done" that drives the saints forward in taking dominion of this world.

> *But the saints of the most High shall take the kingdom, and possess the kingdom for ever, even for ever and ever.*
> *—DANIEL 7:18*

As the Lord has allowed us to minister and travel around the world on His behalf, we have been astonished by the lack of teaching on the subject of discerning the spirit realm. Our prayer is that this book will encourage many to step into the places the Lord has called them. Furthermore, we would desire that this book would act as a guide to help safeguard those who would step out in discerning spirits.

Progressing into the Kingdom

For too long, untold Christians have abided in the wilderness of the natural realm. Scores of believers have never tasted of the goodness of the Kingdom of God. Jesus scolded the Pharisees for not entering the Kingdom and for not permitting others to enter as well.

But woe unto you, scribes and Pharisees, hypocrites! for ye shut up the kingdom of heaven against men: for ye neither go in yourselves, neither suffer ye them that are entering to go in.
—MATTHEW 23:13

When we study the words that Jesus spoke in the New Testament, we discover that He preached repeatedly about the Kingdom of God and the Kingdom of Heaven. Jesus' message was not exclusively focused on salvation. The Lord wants everyone to accept Him as Savior, but He also desires that we cross the threshold into His Father's Kingdom and not just stand at the door. Jesus knew that only as we enter the Kingdom of Heaven can we progress in gaining our inheritance and ruling as His sons.

But as many as received him, to them gave he power to become the sons of God, even to them that believe on his name: *—JOHN 1:12*

And if children, then heirs; heirs of God, and joint-heirs with Christ; if so be that we suffer with him, that we may be also glorified together. *—ROMANS 8:17*

The eyes of your understanding being enlightened; that ye may know what is the hope of his calling, and what the riches of the glory of his inheritance in the saints,
—EPHESIANS 1:18

Numerous believers have utilized the principles you are about to read. The methods are not complicated, but they do require you to allow the Lord to stir and activate your spirit. The apostle Paul encouraged the youthful pastor, Timothy, in this very way.

Wherefore I put thee in remembrance that thou stir up the gift of God, which is in thee by the putting on of my hands.
—*2 TIMOTHY 1:6*

One of the easiest ways to begin stirring up your spirit is to pray in divers tongues. The Word says that we are to pray without ceasing. As you go through your day, pray in the spirit. It does not necessarily have to be out loud where everybody hears you, but can be simply spoken under your breath. The more time you spend keeping your spirit stirred, the less influence your soulish nature is going to have in your life. As your spirit is regularly stirred, you will discover that discernment will come naturally.

So much of discernment is learning how to be tuned into the Lord. The typical believer's life is cluttered with distractions from their jobs, families and the many cares of this world. The enemy wants our focus to be anywhere, except on the Lord. As you pray in the spirit, the Lord will activate your discernment so that you can sense what He is doing around you. Our prayer is that the Lord will stir the gift of discernment within you. As this happens, it will allow the Lord to make Himself known to you in ways beyond anything you could have conceived.

Intimacy

One of the dangers of walking in the realms of the spirit is the tendency to get fascinated with what is going on around us in the spirit realm and not pursue the Lord. We have seen very gifted seers[i] caught up in the gifting they were given. Often, these very gifted ones will allow the things they see and perceive to overcome them.

Watchmen[ii] seem to be particularly susceptible to distraction. They have to be very vigilant to not allow the things they see and perceive to influence them. We have witnessed many watchman get overloaded with such an abundance of sensory input that they lost their effectiveness. They may see a spirit that would want to cause division in the body, and instead of alerting leadership and returning to their place of intercession, they would allow this divisive spirit to take hold of them. The watchman may start becoming divisive himself. Watchmen must continue to go after the Lord through intercession to maintain the contrite heart necessary to flow in the things God has asked of them.

There is also a tendency for watchmen to become lone rangers; because of the things they see and experience, they are often considered strange to others. The enemy hates their giftings and will do everything he can to isolate them from the body. Watchmen must be aware of this enemy tactic and guard themselves against this response.

Intercessors must be careful, too. The Lord will show many things to intercessors as they seek His heart. At the same time, however, the enemy will try to deceive them by infiltrating prayer times with alternative visions and impressions that are extremely convincing.

Our hearts must be melded to the Lord's heart. We want to encourage everyone to seek the gift of discerning of spirits. On the other hand, we would not want you to become infatuated by all the things you see and perceive at the expense of losing that intimacy you must maintain with the Lord.

After my dramatic encounter with the Lord at the Brownsville Revival, I came home both a different pastor and husband. There were many changes that came into my life. One of the things I did was commit my life to interceding on behalf of the Father's purposes. I gave up many areas of ministry I had been involved in and just prayed. As I did, He began showing me many things in the spirit. God graciously opened up many new sights and experiences in both the Heaven of Heavens and in the second heavens. On an almost daily basis, the Lord took me on visits to different and incredibly wonderful places in the spirit realm. Angels visited regularly during daily prayer times.

However, after a few years of almost unbelievable revelation, this gift of sight began to fade. Visions and experiences came less and less frequently. Uncertainty and doubt began to creep in. There was no explanation for why I was experiencing less and less in the spirit realm. I could not find anything different in my daily routine of prayer and intercession and there were no known sins to blame. Daily experiences became weekly and eventually monthly. Then months at a time would pass without seeing or experiencing anything at all in the spirit.

I was doing my very best to not become discouraged. I regularly fought jealousy as others within my church were continuing to see things. Here I was, one of the leaders, and my vision was diminishing. Even though I felt like I was starting to fall behind, the

Lord was telling me He wanted me to start teaching others how to walk in the mighty gifting of discerning of spirits.

The Lord also told me during this season that He wanted to hone my skills in discernment in ways that I had not yet experienced. God made it very clear that He did not want me to allow jealousy or discouragement to slow down my progress. A very essential point He was making was that He did not want the pursuit of seeing things in the spirit to take precedence over my pursing Him. I had become addicted to the thrill of seeing things in the spirit. The Lord wanted me addicted to Him and only Him. God is very concerned with the passion and focus of His children.

Please do not misunderstand me, seeing in the spirit is wonderful and we encourage this gifting in believers. However at this particular time, the Lord needed to teach me how to keep Him first in my heart.

Over the last several years the Lord has taught me a great deal about intimacy with Him. I have learned to know when He has come and what happens in me when that occurs. I definitely miss some of the amazing experiences that I used to have, but I would not trade all the visions in the world for the relationship with the Lord that has developed over these last several years.

I am perfectly content if I never see another thing in the spirit or ever again perceive an angel. I must have the Lord. I must know Him more. There is no spiritual gift or miraculous ministry that we should ever allow to come between the Lord and ourselves. Are you willing to give up everything, everything spiritual and even good, to know Him more deeply?

Most of us know about the book of Song of Solomon. It is one of the books of the Bible that many pass by because of the graphic and somewhat embarrassing terminology Solomon uses. However, within this powerful book are the secrets to greater intimacy with the Lord.

Spiritual Senses

The Lord wants to teach us how to discern with our spiritual senses. This will enable us to experience Him in ways that defy description. I was also amazed as I examined the Song of Solomon to see how each of our natural senses is individually described. We must want to know the Lord in a way beyond what we have experienced thus far. We must want the Lord to activate our spiritual capacities to know Him more intimately.

As you read the following passages, ask the Lord to activate in your spirit the particular spiritual sense that is represented.

Taste

*Let him kiss me with the **kisses of his mouth**: for thy love is better than wine.* —*SONG OF SOLOMON 1:2*

*As the apple tree among the trees of the wood, so is my beloved among the sons. I sat down under his shadow with great delight, and his fruit was **sweet to my taste.***
—SONG OF SOLOMON 2:3

*Thy lips, O my spouse, drop as the honeycomb: honey and milk are **under thy tongue**; and the smell of thy garments is like the smell of Lebanon.* —*SONG OF SOLOMON 4:11*

*And the roof of thy mouth like the best wine for my beloved, that goeth down sweetly, causing the **lips** of those that are asleep to speak.* —*SONG OF SOLOMON 7:9*

Sight

***Look** not upon me, because I am black, because the sun hath **looked** upon me: my mother's children were angry with me; they made me the keeper of the vineyards; but mine own vineyard have I not kept.*
—SONG OF SOLOMON 1:6

*My beloved is like a roe or a young hart: behold, he standeth behind our wall, he **looketh** forth at the windows, shewing himself through the lattice.*
—SONG OF SOLOMON 2:9

*O my dove, that art in the clefts of the rock, in the secret places of the stairs, let me **see** thy countenance, let me hear thy voice; for sweet is thy voice, and thy countenance is comely.*
—SONG OF SOLOMON 2:14

Smell

While the king sitteth at his table, my spikenard sendeth forth the smell thereof
—*SONG OF SOLOMON 1:12*

The fig tree putteth forth her green figs, and the vines with the tender grape give a good smell. Arise, my love, my fair one, and come away.
—*SONG OF SOLOMON 2:13*

Who is this that cometh out of the wilderness like pillars of smoke, perfumed with myrrh and frankincense, with all powders of the merchant?
—*SONG OF SOLOMON 3:6*

How fair is thy love, my sister, my spouse! how much better is thy love than wine! and the smell of thine ointments than all spices!
—*SONG OF SOLOMON 4:10*

Hearing

The flowers appear on the earth; the time of the singing of birds is come, and the voice of the turtle is heard in our land;
—*SONG OF SOLOMON 2:12*

O my dove, that art in the clefts of the rock, in the secret places of the stairs, let me see thy countenance, let me hear thy voice; for sweet is thy voice, and thy countenance is comely.
—*SONG OF SOLOMON 2:14*

I sleep, but my heart waketh: it is the voice of my beloved that knocketh, saying, Open to me, my sister, my love, my dove, my undefiled: for my head is filled with dew, and my locks with the drops of the night.
—*SONG OF SOLOMON 5:2*

Thou that dwellest in the gardens, the companions hearken to thy voice: cause me to hear it.
—*SONG OF SOLOMON 8:13*

Touch

His left hand is under my head, and his right hand doth
embrace *me.* ———*SONG OF SOLOMON 2:6*

*It was but a little that I passed from them, but I found him
whom my soul loveth: I **held** him, and would not let him go,
until I had brought him into my mother's house, and into the
chamber of her that conceived me.*
———*SONG OF SOLOMON 3:4*

The Gift of Discerning of Spirits

The reality of what it actually means to walk in the Spirit is
surrounded by many misconceptions. We have spent most of our lives
learning about the Bible and the Lord, hoping that it would draw us
closer to Him. Instead we have become experts on the topic of God,
but do not personally know Him. The primary goal of most churches
is to get people saved and to make sure their congregations have a
good head-knowledge of the Bible. Each type of church or
denomination expects its congregants to follow its own specific rules
of appropriate behavior. For many Christians, finding a ministry in a
church, and being faithful to it, is their way of walking in the Spirit.

If we live in the Spirit, let us also walk in the Spirit.
———*GALATIANS 5:25*

We did our very best to live a Christian life that pleased the
Lord, our family and the church. Unfortunately, we struggled through
many frustrating years as we learned the hard way that our efforts had
very little effect on our abilities to draw closer to the Lord. What
finally changed this picture was when the Lord intervened and brought
a radical point of dying to our own efforts. In that process He taught
us how to live in Him and that the soulish nature must be relinquished
to Him. He taught us how to allow our spirit man to take control
instead of our soulish man.

How tragic it is to lead someone to the saving knowledge of
Christ Jesus and only fill them with knowledge about God. The church
often fails to teach them how to have a personal relationship with God.
The good news of the gospel must be followed up with the reality of
what it means to walk with the Lord and what it means to really know
the Lord.

The point is that you cannot learn enough scripture or live a perfect enough life to be worthy to flow in discernment. **Discernment is a gift.** All we must do to receive the gift of discerning of spirits is to simply ask Him for it.

> *And whatsoever we ask, we receive of him, because we keep his commandments, and do those things that are pleasing in his sight.* —1 JOHN 3:22

> *So that ye come behind in no gift; waiting for the coming of our Lord Jesus Christ:* —1 CORINTHIANS 1:7

Truthfully, we know numerous people who have received this wonderful gift without ever asking for it. The Lord loves His children and He undoubtedly recognizes that discernment is an indispensable gift for the saints in these last days. Our Heavenly Father is making sure we are equipped to cope with the challenges that are ahead.

Defining Discernment

Before we continue our study of discernment, it would be wise to define it. Essentially, to discern means to separate, distinguish between, to sift, or to detect with senses other than vision. Basically, it is not relying on our physical senses to discern spiritual matters.

If we are not careful, our discernment can get mixed with our preferences, logical thinking, opinions, and emotions. Discernment should also not be mistaken for suspicion. Suspicion is to have doubt or mistrust about someone. It is to secretly look at or spy on someone in a clandestine manner. It is to imagine one guilty without proof or substantiation. Spiritual discernment emanates from the Holy Spirit. It is supernatural knowledge, perception or sight given to bring us to the truth. In truth, discernment knows without having evidence.

> *And the spirit of the Lord shall rest upon him, the spirit of wisdom and understanding, the spirit of counsel and might, the spirit of knowledge and of the fear of the Lord; ³And shall make him of quick understanding in the fear of the Lord: and he shall not judge after the sight of his eyes, neither reprove after the hearing of his ears:* —ISAIAH 11:2-3

> *Beloved, believe not every spirit, but try the spirits whether they are of God: because many false prophets are gone out into the world.* —*1 JOHN 4:1*

Soulish discernment is normally based on physical hints. In our minds, we often accept these hints as factual evidence, when in fact they are not. As humans, our first instinct is to filter things that we see in the natural through our minds. This is a major mistake. We cannot trust our natural eyes. The Bible says our minds need to be renewed.

> *And be not conformed to this world: but be ye transformed by the **renewing** of your mind, that ye may prove what is that good, and acceptable, and perfect, will of God.* —*ROMANS 12:2*

> *And be **renewed** in the spirit of your mind;* —*EPHESIANS 4:23*

Given man's tendency to base his judgment and decision-making on guesses about physical evidence, there is great potential for error. If we were operating in our discernment correctly, we would not be making these kinds of mistakes. The Holy Spirit does not guess, He knows.

We have encountered situations in worship services all over the world when someone will begin screaming during the service. In the natural, this is both startling and troubling. This situation used to truly concern us. Our immediate soulish thoughts were that this person must be demonized. However, the Lord began to teach us that instead of judging with our natural abilities we needed to discern what was actually going on in the spirit realm. Sometimes these are demonic outbursts, but often the root-cause is simply emotional. Many times people who are carrying emotional baggage can react to the presence of the Lord in very unusual ways. Often their behavior is misinterpreted as demonic when in reality it is just strange behavior. The crying out is more an emotional release than a demonic manifestation. The Lord wants to teach us to discern immediately the real cause of the manifestation.

It might be wise as you grow in your discernment to earmark those who function mightily in this gift. In those cases where there is uncertainty, it is good to have others assist with the determination of what is happening in the spirit.

But he that is spiritual judgeth all things, yet he himself is judged of no man.   *1 CORINTHIANS 2:15*

---

[i] Seers are individuals whose foundational spiritual contribution to the Kingdom of God is to perceive things in the spirit realm. An Old Testament term, the companion New Testament function is the Teacher. Both perceive with understanding the context of what is happening in the spiritual realm at a particular juncture point.

[ii] Watchmen are individuals whose function within the body of Christ is one of watching for and warning of enemy attacks.

Discerning the Kingdom of God

2

Soulish Nature

The Word is very clear that man is made up of body, soul and spirit.

*And the very God of peace sanctify you wholly; and I pray God your whole **spirit** and **soul** and **body** be preserved blameless unto the coming of our Lord Jesus Christ.*
—1 THESSOLONIANS 5:23

There are many good studies which would provide you with a greater depth of knowledge on this subject. For example, Watchman Nee has done a masterful job of articulating this subject.

First we must address the soulish nature. This is an area that can cause great confusion and even destruction in an individual if it is not dealt with properly. When we accept Jesus Christ as our Savior, our spirit man is born again. We become new creatures in Christ. We now have the capacity to know and worship the Lord. As part of our new birth, we are promised eternal life and eventually new bodies. On the other hand, our soul is not born again. It requires a progressive work by the Lord, and it really never gets fully perfected while we are here on this earth. The Word teaches that our soulish nature must be renewed.

And be not conformed to this world: but be ye transformed by the renewing of your mind, that ye may prove what is that good, and acceptable, and perfect, will of God.
—ROMANS 12:2

Dealing with Iniquities

The blood that was shed on the cross was for the forgiveness of our sins. However, there is difference between sin, which can be forgiven, and iniquity. Sin is the committing of an offense against the laws of God. The word sin actually means to miss the mark. Jesus said that even contemplating committing sin was a sin.

Ye have heard that it was said by them of old time, Thou shalt not commit adultery: 28But I say unto you, That whosoever looketh on a woman to lust after her hath committed adultery with her already in his heart.

—MATTHEW 5:27-28

On the other hand, iniquity means a twisting. Iniquity is that twisting in us that leads us toward sin. Many times there are iniquities that are still very much at work in our lives even though we have accepted Jesus as Lord and Savior. Iniquities[iii] are a twisting of our original purpose. Iniquities can be caused by generational sins or even by demonic influences. Iniquities lead us to sin. The enemy tries to cause the iniquity within us to rise up. This hinders the flow of gifts and abilities God has placed within us.

Many churches stress evangelism. Bookstores are full of reading material designed to help the church accomplish the "great commission". Salvation is the process by which our spirits are regenerated. In some churches, once a person is saved they are encouraged to get filled with the Spirit. Beyond this, most young believers are left to struggle with bad habits and sins that have always plagued them. Rarely do you ever hear teaching that explains why there are still tremendous obstacles to overcome even after we are saved. Many people tend to live out their lives with a lot of guilt or frustration, because they have not overcome areas of weakness.

There are many believers who try to operate in the gifts of the Spirit while also living with unresolved issues from the past. These issues usually can be traced back either to generational sins, the need for inner healing from circumstances in the past, or deliverance from habitual sins. God is continuously dealing with our hearts. He desires to have pure vessels to minister through. One of the hardest things for many Christians to realize is that evil spirits can reside on or even in them. If you have had some difficult past experiences that you have not been healed from – get healing. If we do not deal with these iniquities, they will cause our discernment to be inaccurate. We have seen many people make the crucial error of misidentifying dark angels as the Lord's angels because of these iniquitous issues in their lives that skew their discernment.

Remember King Saul, who after operating in the godly prophetic early in his life, because he allowed jealousy and other unresolved iniquities to remain in him, actually turns to a woman with a familiar spirit at the end of his life.

As we begin committing ourselves to prayer, the Lord is very gracious to begin dealing with iniquities which have rooted themselves deep within us. We learn from the Apostle Paul that we must die daily (1 Corinthians 15:31). It is not a matter of acting more holy; rather it is a matter of God doing something within our hearts that changes us. As we allow Him to increase in our lives and we put to death our soulish and fleshly natures so that we decrease, we will begin seeing a lot of those things that held us back broken off of our lives.

The Lord had to deal with the issue of jealousy in my own life. If it had not been dealt with properly, then my discernment could be distorted and faulty. This is just one of many potential challenges that come with having to deal with our soulish nature.

Jesus spoke of this truth when He talked about the mote and the beam.

And why beholdest thou the mote that is in thy brother's eye, but <u>considerest not the beam that is in thine own eye?</u> ⁴Or how wilt thou say to thy brother, Let me pull out the mote out of thine eye; and, behold, a beam is in thine own eye? ⁵Thou hypocrite, <u>first cast out the beam out of thine own eye; and then shalt thou see clearly</u> to cast out the mote out of thy brother's eye. —MATTHEW 7:3-5

Composition of the Soul

Unfortunately, most discernment is based on the perspective of our soulish man. The more the soulish realm has control of you, the less accurate your discernment will be. We must understand that God wants us to discern from the perspective of His Spirit.

The soul is composed of the will, intellect, emotions, imagination and memory. The will is used to express desire, choice, willingness, consent; and to express frequent, customary, or habitual action or natural tendency or disposition. It is also used to express determination, insistence, persistence, or willfulness.

Intellect: The intellect is the power of knowing as distinguished from the power to feel or to will. It is also the capacity for knowledge and for rational or intelligent thought especially when highly developed. With the many facets that compose our souls, we must be careful that these elements do not corrupt our spiritual discernment. The enemy will try to get you to lean on your natural intellect instead of using the mind of Christ. Many times we do not honestly consider the source of our assessment in a situation and simply rely on our natural reasoning abilities. Once we make up our minds, we are then determined to prove ourselves right in a situation and impose our wills to defend our position. This kind of attitude will hamper our ability to discern clearly. We must be willing to not understand something intellectually. God said His ways appear foolish to man. God's ways can only be spiritually discerned.

But the natural man receiveth not the things of the Spirit of God: for they are foolishness unto him: neither can he know them, because they are spiritually discerned.
—1 CORINTHIANS 2:14

Memory: Memory is the power or process of reproducing or recalling what has been learned and retained especially through associative mechanisms. Memory represents the accumulation of things learned and retained from prior activity or experience. We must be very careful not to allow past memories to influence our discernment. You cannot allow things that you remember about someone or about a similar situation to influence your present discernment. Honestly, it is very difficult to accurately discern things about individuals or situations close to you.

Remember ye not the former things, neither consider the things of old. 19Behold, I will do a new thing; now it shall spring forth; shall ye not know it? I will even make a way in the wilderness, and rivers in the desert.
—ISAIAH 43:18-19

Imagination: The imagination is the act or power of forming a mental image of something not present to the senses or never before wholly perceived in reality. Our imaginations, if not disciplined, can be a major deterrent in discerning accurately. Most people are not adept at distinguishing between their own imaginations and spiritual perceptions. It is very dangerous to utilize your imagination instead of learning how to glean what the spirit is showing. Often we recognize too late that someone has professed a word or revelation is from the Lord when it is in reality only a product of their own imagination. Some people tend to naturally have ongoing images flash across their minds. It is absolutely necessary to bring our thoughts into the subjection of the Holy Spirit.

> *Casting down imaginations, and every high thing that exalteth itself against the knowledge of God, and bringing into captivity every thought to the obedience of Christ;*
> *—2 CORINTHIANS 10:5*

God is pleased with those who allow the Lord total control of their thoughts and imaginations. He blesses those who will humble themselves before Him; those who are always seeking in prayer to really know His voice, and not just trusting every thought that comes into their minds. The Lord is very clear about what He thinks of and how He judges those who claim to speak for Him and are actually lying. Notice how Jeremiah speaks of their "lightness", which means to treat lightly or with disregard to the seriousness of speaking falsely (Jeremiah 14:14, 29:9). This verse implies that the telling of false dreams or words does not have to be intentional, but could be the result of careless disregard for the process of knowing whether or not something is actually from the Lord.

> *Behold, I am against them that prophesy false dreams, saith the LORD, and do tell them, and cause my people to err by their lies, and by their lightness; yet I sent them not, nor commanded them: therefore they shall not profit this people at all, saith the LORD.* —*JEREMIAH 23:32*

Emotions: The final area of our soul that we need to address is our emotions. Emotions affect every area of our consciousness. They represent our feelings and produce both mental and physical reactions. Emotions have the most direct affect from the natural realm on our discernment. According to medical science, all of our sensory perceptions of taste, touch, smell, hearing and sight, go through the emotional center of the brain first. They then reach the thinking center of the brain where thoughts, ideas and understanding reside. People who do not learn to or choose not to control their emotions are at the mercy of their feelings. This is the reason why so many people give way to emotional outbursts which range from taking offense and internalizing rejection to exploding in rage and committing heinous crimes.

Our soulish man is extremely sensitive to external stimuli and our enemy knows it. Sometimes in order to prepare us for His Kingdom and to refine us, the Lord may allow us to go through a seemingly hopeless situation. Abraham, Moses, David and Job all faced situations where there seemed to be no hope. Remember, the Lord does not tempt man with evil (James 1:13-14). It is man who is drawn by his own lust (emotional desires) to sin. Our enemy is crafty. He will recognize an opportunity and attack you with discouragement or even depression. Demonic spirits will work in a coordinated fashion to launch assaults that directly target our emotions. If we are not careful, we can be overwhelmed by feelings of hopelessness or fear. The key to overcoming these attacks is to not allow the thoughts or feelings to linger for any length of time. It could spell disaster if you do not take immediate action. Remind yourself of the promises that are in the Word of God. At these pivotal times, we must press into the Lord and listen to what He is saying. This is often a challenge, because the enemy's voice is loud, and the intensity of our own emotions often reinforce the enemy's words. You must remember that perception is not reality. Believe the report of the Lord, not your own perceptions or your emotional response to these perceptions.

Another ploy of the enemy is to attack our emotions through some offense or sense of injustice. Our normal reaction is to allow a root of bitterness to grow. That bitterness will trigger anger and all manner of evil speaking and thinking will follow. Often these offenses come by way of those we love very dearly. We have lost count of the times that people have done or said something that was like an arrow shooting in us in the back. There was such a temptation to lash back or even cut them off, but the Lord would not permit me to do either one.

If bitterness is not dealt with, it can do permanent damage to our ability to minister out of a pure heart. Jesus continually spoke about forgiving those that persecute and attack us without a cause (Matthew 5:11). It is paramount that our hearts stay pure or our ability to see into the realms of the spirit without being deceived will be greatly hindered.

Blessed are the pure in heart: for they shall see God.
—*MATTHEW 5:8*

22

Let all bitterness, and wrath, and anger, and clamour, and evil speaking, be put away from you, with all malice:
                                                            —EPHESIANS 4:31

But if ye have bitter envying and strife in your hearts, glory not, and lie not against the truth.   *—JAMES 3:14*

Deceiving and Being Deceived

One of the key reasons for this controlling of our emotions, or dying to self, is so that we do not allow our emotions to control us. This will prevent deception. Notice that James says bitterness is rooted in envy and breeds strife, pride and lies. Constantly throughout scripture we are warned to avoid being deceived.

But evil men and seducers shall wax worse and worse, **deceiving***, and being* **deceived***.*
                                                            —2 TIMOTHY 3:13

And Jesus answered and said unto them, Take heed that no man **deceive** *you.*   *—MATTHEW 24:4*

Do not lightly read through these verses. There are some critical aspects to deception that it is imperative that we see. First of all, we must beware of being deceived by others. This would indicate someone else is intentionally "tricking" us into believing a lie. When it comes to discernment, one of the most deadly errors is to base your discernment on what others have told you. That is not discernment. It is suspicion.

For there shall arise false Christs, and false prophets, and shall shew great signs and wonders; insomuch that, if it were possible, they shall **deceive** *the very elect.*
                                                            —MATTHEW 24:24

Secondly, there is a false anointing (false Christs) and a false prophetic that will try to deceive you. This is fueled by the enemy. Just because you perceive something in the spirit realm, it does not make it truth. The enemy will show you visions, signs, wonders, dreams, and revelations that appear to be from God. They do not come with a "Made in Hell" tag.

For sin, taking occasion by the commandment, deceived me, and by it slew me.   *—ROMANS 7:11*

Some of the saddest stories we can tell you are about the many gifted seers and prophets we know who believe everything they see in the spirit realm. Early in their spiritual walk they were careful to try the spirits. However, after several encounters with godly angels they began to believe they could "tell the difference". Pride came in subtly, and they began to believe that no fallen angel could deceive them. Sadly, that is exactly what did happen. Slowly but surely, through visits from fallen angels seen in dreams and visions, iniquity began to twist them. Now blatant sin is considered acceptable. These dear ones have been deceived into believing one of Satan's most effective lines, to equate spiritual experience with godly approval.

But be ye doers of the word, and not hearers only, deceiving your own selves.   *—JAMES 1:22*

If any man among you seem to be religious, and bridleth not his tongue, but deceiveth his own heart, this man's religion is vain.   *—JAMES 1:26*

This is one of the biggest lies the enemy uses against the elect. History shows how many great men of God through the ages have fallen into sin. The very sins they had preached against captured them. Why? It was because they believed the lie that equates spiritual experience or spiritual power with godly approval. God's approval is only bestowed on obedient, humble sons who are pure in heart. His gifts are without repentance, so having received a spiritual gift of sight, He does not take it away when you fall into sin. This is evidenced by the many gifted individuals who have dedicated their giftings to the enemy's camp. Mind readers, sorcerers, witches, mediums all operate in spiritual giftings. That does not make them godly!

Let no man deceive himself. If any man among you seemeth to be wise in this world, let him become a fool, that he may be wise.   *—1 CORINTHIANS 3:18*

Satan is the Father of Lies. He is a master at creating just the right atmosphere and backdrop to make what he tells you appear to be the truth. Everything, absolutely everything that comes from God will align with the scriptures. This is absolute truth, but even in this test there is a loophole that the enemy employs with great success. It is possible for the enemy to find scriptural support for almost anything.

Remember how Satan tried to twist scripture when tempting our Lord Jesus in the wilderness. Consider this modern day example. There were those who wholeheartedly believed they were mandated by God and commissioned by His Word to commit the atrocities of World War II in Nazi Germany. One of the men tried and found guilty at the Nuremburg trials for creating the propaganda backdrop to justify Hitler's ethnic cleansing of the Jews, the Gypsies, and the handicapped, was also the author of a New Testament Greek Lexicon that is used widely by Christians still today. This fits the 2 Timothy 3:13 warning about deceiving and being deceived. This gifted scholar knew God's Word well, but did not know the God of His Word.

The final aspect of deception is when you deceive yourself. If you base your beliefs on your feelings, on what you wish were true, on your desires or opinions, or on offences you have taken up, your discernment will not be accurate and you will deceive yourself. This is so central to the fallen nature of man. We could name a dozen self-deceptions that we see in the carnal world every day: addicts who do not believe they are addicts, abusive parents or spouses who do not believe their behavior is wrong, murderers who justify their crimes to themselves and others. Self-deception is so easy.

The only cure is meekness and humility. You must submit everything you perceive to the Lord and to the authority structure under which God has placed you. You must be willing to have every prophetic word, every dream or vision judged by the spiritual ones around you. The judges themselves must be judged. No one is exempt. That is why scripture so clearly speaks of both judging yourself and judging others. It takes great humility to say to yourself, "I could be wrong, only the Lord knows, and He will reveal the truth in due time."

*Let the prophets speak two or three, and let the other **judge**.*
—*1 CORINTHIANS 14:29*

Anger Blinds

Remember we spoke of how Jesus told us to forgive those that persecute and attack us. It is paramount that our hearts stay pure or our ability to see into the realms of the spirit without being deceived will be greatly hindered. It is also imperative that we not dwell in anger.

Blessed are ye, when men shall revile you, and persecute you, and shall say all manner of evil against you falsely, for my sake. ^{12}Rejoice, and be exceeding glad: for great is your reward in heaven: for so persecuted they the prophets which were before you. —MATTHEW 5:11-12

Rest in the LORD, and wait patiently for him: fret not thyself because of him who prospereth in his way, because of the man who bringeth wicked devices to pass. ^{8}Cease from anger, and forsake wrath: fret not thyself in any wise to do evil. —PSALMS 37:7-8

Be not hasty in thy spirit to be angry: for anger resteth in the bosom of fools. —ECCLESIATES 7:9

He that is slow to anger is better than the mighty; and he that ruleth his spirit than he that taketh a city. —PROVERBS 16:32

Let all bitterness, and wrath, and anger, and clamour, and evil speaking, be put away from you, with all malice: —EPHESIANS 4:31

When you cannot control your anger, it is a good indication that your soul is too sensitive and that you have pride in your heart. There is a righteous anger. One example of righteous anger would be when Jesus threw over the tables of the moneychangers in the Temple. God spoke of His anger with the wicked and with those who turned their back on Him. However, we know both our Lord Jesus Christ and our Father God do not sin. The Apostle Paul even said, "Be angry and sin not." We know God does not get angry because of pride or selfishness. Unfortunately, if we are honest with ourselves, the source of our anger is usually one or both of these evil motives. We must be walking in such a way with the Lord that nothing really riles us up or fazes us. The Lord is at peace all the time. We must ask the Lord to give us this kind of supernatural peace that does not react to people's words or actions.

Peace I leave with you, my peace I give unto you: not as the world giveth, give I unto you. Let not your heart be troubled, neither let it be afraid. —JOHN 14:27

The enemy was constantly probing Jesus, trying to find areas where he could antagonize Him. Jesus was placed in some very pressurized situations, yet He always responded with such grace and gentleness. Jesus was all about doing His Father's will. If in doing His Father's will, those close to Him came against Him, then so be it. He always looked from the perspective of how His Father wanted things done. If anger was part of the will of His Father, then He stepped into that flow with the Spirit of Judgment and Burning. However, there are many more examples of Jesus demonstrating great restraint when anger would have been the most common reaction.

There are far more situations that call for us to be quiet and still our emotions than situations where God would approve of us exploding in anger. Our reaction to a situation means a great deal to the Lord. We represent Him. If He is abiding in us, then we need to allow His response to flow through us.

Do Not Compare With Others

One of the most effective devices the enemy has in his arsenal is his ability to speak thoughts into a person. His list of destructive thoughts is immense. However, the thought that you have been overlooked is an especially potent poison. Often this happens when a person desires a position or promotion within the body. A person may feel they deserve the recognition for their gifting and spiritual maturity. They may covet the ways in which many others around them have received. When this recognition is not forthcoming, a strong sense of self-pity begins its evil work.

It is not very long until this individual is watching and comparing themselves to everyone. They begin taking great care to notice even the slightest hint that they are being left out or passed over. All along, the Lord is trying to remind them about the danger of "comparing themselves among themselves." If a person does not deal with these thoughts and feelings appropriately, they will be overcome by them.

For we dare not make ourselves of the number, or compare ourselves with some that commend themselves: but they measuring themselves by themselves, and comparing themselves among themselves, are not wise.
—2 CORINTHIANS 10:12

27

It is not long until the same person is looking for others to join their pity party. They begin to poison others with the poison into which they have themselves bitten. Those who have strong mercy giftings are targets for those who are flowing in self-pity. It is amazing how the enemy can absolutely blind a person to the truth when they are flowing in self-pity.

Often these individuals will get so angry that they leave the church. Please understand these individuals are wonderful believers who move powerfully in the gifts of God. However, they have not taken their thoughts captive. Instead, they have listened to the thoughts sent out by the enemy. The enemy's agents of deception are powerful. You must identify and deal with them before they cause you to abort the perfect purposes of God in your life.

Self-pity or actually self-anything, is a death knell to discernment. It is a loud, persistent noise that totally drowns out the voice of God. God said, *"Be still, and know that I am God."* When our self-nature is rising up and clamoring for attention, our discernment will be distorted.

Turning Deaf Ears to Criticism

Criticism or fear of criticism is another weapon in our enemy's arsenal. Our natural reaction is to avoid criticism anyway we can. Criticism can cause us to think twice about whether what God told us to do is really worth doing or whether we really heard Him correctly. The primary targets of criticism are leaders in the Lord's Kingdom. Notice how crafty the enemy is, he will often stir up one minister to criticize another minister. We cannot criticize others, nor can we allow those that would criticize our efforts to hinder us from moving forward. God is calling forth His saints to lead the way in taking dominion of this planet. Part of walking with the Lord is to be subjected to criticism. Jesus warned us that this is just the way it is.

Blessed are ye, when men shall revile you, and persecute you, and shall say all manner of evil against you falsely, for my sake. —MATTHEW 5:11

If the world hate you, ye know that it hated me before it hated you. —JOHN 15:18

None of us enjoy criticism, but unfortunately it will come. When faced with criticism our temptation is to withdraw, or we may be tempted to strike back with our own harsh words. This is never a healthy solution. We must remember what Jesus and the apostles said about reviling words.

> *Speak not evil one of another, brethren. He that speaketh evil of his brother, and judgeth his brother, speaketh evil of the law, and judgeth the law: but if thou judge the law, thou art not a doer of the law, but a judge. [12]There is one lawgiver, who is able to save and to destroy: who art thou that judgest another?* —JAMES 4:11-12

> *And labour, working with our own hands: being reviled, we bless; being persecuted, we suffer it:*
> —1 CORINTHIANS 4:12

> *Who, when he was reviled, reviled not again; when he suffered, he threatened not; but committed himself to him that judgeth righteously:* —1 PETER 2:23

Make Your Soul Subject To Your Spirit

Ultimately, the Lord wants our souls to be subject to His Spirit. He wants our spirits moving in sync with His Spirit. As the strength of our spirit man increases, we will find our soulish man has less influence. The Word says that Christ is to be formed in us. Daily, this process is taking place as we submit to the Lord. It is through continual intercession and the act of placing our hearts and lives before Him that we are changed.

Simply put, our souls need to be changed and renewed. God created our souls to function with our spirits, but being unredeemed, it takes time. In doctrinal terms, this process is called "progressive sanctification". This change will take great patience on our part. However, the quicker we submit to the Lord's process, the sooner we will begin to see major changes in our lives.

Be Wise in Your Discernment

A wonderful example of why our souls must be surrendered to God is played out when we actually discern something. As you begin to discern, you must exercise great wisdom and patience as to how and when to act on your discernment.

As your discernment increases, you tend to sense more demonic activity in and around people. Sensing the demonic is not the same as receiving an instruction from the Lord to do anything other than pray for His will to be done. Pray for God to deliver us from evil. That is what Jesus taught us to do. Sensing the demonic especially does not mean you are to tell the person involved what you are sensing, nor to encourage immediate deliverance. Often God will not want you to reveal what He has shown you. It is absolutely imperative that we DO NOT act on our discernment until the Lord tells us to do so. The most important thing to discern is what God is saying in a situation and what He wants done. Inevitably, the first and most important thing that God wants you to do about what He has revealed to you is to pray.

It all goes back to having an intimate relationship with the Lord. We must know His voice. God is much more concerned about His perfect timing than releasing information or doing some form of ministry. Jesus said we always are ready to say, "it is time", but Jesus actually discerned and waited for God's timing.

Then Jesus said unto them, My time is not yet come: but your time is alway ready.

—JOHN 7:6

Another word of wisdom; it is best not to discuss with others what you have discerned on or around someone else. You should only speak of your spiritual perceptions to someone in your leadership who has been designated to receive and deal with this type of revelation from the Lord. Spiritual perception is not for the purpose of showing off your ability to perceive. It is for the purpose of praying for the Father's will to be done. The first thing we do when we perceive anything is pray about it, and pray for discernment to know if there is anything else we should do about it. Always pray first! Pray for God's Kingdom to be established in that person, for His will to be done, for His grace and peace to flow in that life.

Be careful that when you perceive something, you do not accuse others. The Word teaches us about not judging others. If God shows something about another person, it is for you to have His heart toward that one.

We must also be careful not to become obstinate in our opinions. Our minds are quick to jump to conclusions and soulish interpretations about what we have perceived. We need to have our hearts broken and contrite before the Lord.

30

The Lord is nigh unto them that are of a broken heart; and saveth such as be of a contrite spirit.

—PSALM 34:18

We should never be too harsh when dealing with people. Through the discernment the Lord gives us, we may pick up on many negative aspects of others' lives. We are not their judge and jury. Our hearts must be full of His love and we must flow in mercy. The Lord in most cases is very gentle when He deals with us. We must ask Him for this same kind of gentleness in our hearts when we consider what He has shown us about others.

Sometimes your spirit will discern things that will cause your soul to want to react immediately. Take your time and listen carefully to how God wants you to respond. You will be amazed how much the Lord will show you about His will for the situation. This is all part of our training in knowing the perfect timing of the Lord.

Truly <u>the signs of an apostle were wrought among you in all patience</u>, in signs, and wonders, and mighty deeds.

—2 CORINTHIANS 12:12

All of us want to be apostolic. However, the first sign of the apostolic is not signs and wonders, but patience. The soulish man is by nature impatient. We must ask the Lord to teach us to not get ahead of His timing. The moment we get ahead of God, we are moving in the flesh. Once you are moving in the flesh, you are not flowing in the discernment that is from the Lord.

Pray for the stilling of your soul. The Apostle Paul said that the carnal man battles with the spirit man. We must ask on a daily basis for the Lord to increase our spirit man and for the fleshly and soulish natures to decrease. Pray for His perfect peace to abide upon you.

Know the Word

For the word of God is quick, and powerful, and sharper than any twoedged sword, piercing even to the dividing asunder of soul and spirit, and of the joints and marrow, and is a discerner of the thoughts and intents of the heart.

—HEBREWS 4:12

31

We must be students of the Bible to operate effectively in our discernment. The Lord exhorts us to study to know the truth. Our discernment must be based on the Word of God. Every aspect of our discernment must be based on and aligned with the Bible or it becomes carnal in nature.

There are many things being taught in the church world today about heaven and the angels. Many of these teachings sound good and draw us to believe very quickly. However, some of these teachings are based solely on the things that people have perceived in the spirit realm. One stream of ministry reports having seen multiple thrones of God in heaven. They describe where these thrones are located and what transpires in each of these places. Most report these thrones are empty and that God moves around from throne to throne. However, the Bible teaches God has only one Throne in Heaven. You must beware. All spiritual perceptions, no matter how fantastic and anointed they sound, must line up with the scriptures.

This is only one example of twisted spiritual perception. If these individuals operated in the gift of discernment, they would realize they were being shown a lie. We absolutely believe these individuals saw thrones, but according to the scriptures they were not the thrones of God. We have seen many thrones as well, both empty and filled with dark angels. Scriptures even say there are thrones for the elders, but there is only one throne of God. We must be very cautious not to believe every report we hear about the spirit realm. To swallow without study these types of teaching is to be led into deception.

The Word says we need to be careful of the wiles of the devil.

Put on the whole armour of God, that ye may be able to stand against the wiles of the devil.

—EPHESIANS 6:11

Literally, the "wiles of the enemy" are his many ways of tricking the saints. Jesus said over and over again in Matthew 24 that the last days would be characterized by deceptions. The best way to avoid being deceived or being seduced by the enemy is to know the truth. In these perilous times we must be incredibly accurate in our discernment. Our very lives and the lives of those around us could depend upon it.

When we see images of Heaven and of heavenly places, we need to look to the Word of God for validation. When we hear people

32

teach on how we are to access the heavens and God's throne, we need to make sure these prophets and teachers are operating on a solid biblical foundation. Be wary of those that regularly make claims that cannot be supported by the Word.

It is absolutely glorious what God is revealing in the heavens to His children in this hour. He is inviting us to not only see, but to experience these wonderful places He has created for us. He is allowing us to venture into the second heavens and take our places in seats that belong to us. At the same time, however, our experiences must be backed up by His Word. Our discernment must filter through the Word. It does not matter how powerful your spiritual sensors are if you do not distinguish between what is of God, "good", and what is from Satan, "evil". If you cannot discern whether or not your perception lines up with the Word, you are wiser not to share it until God gives you scriptural validation.

The Lord has been very gracious to show us some amazing things in the heavens. We have seen some things that we believe are absolutely real; however, we have not yet been given the revelation from the Word that would validate what was seen. If we have correctly discerned the revelation is from God, in time God will reveal this mystery in His Word. For now, the exercise of patience and a closed mouth is necessary until God clarifies through His Word what has been perceived. Only then will it be the appropriate time to share.

To conclude this chapter on our soulish nature, some would suggest it would be safer to not perceive anything of the spirit realm at all. This is the most ludicrous of thoughts. It is like saying it is better if we are blind and deaf because we might see evil or be enticed to go the wrong way. We are spirit beings, and there is a very real spirit realm of which we are a part, whether we want to be or not. Having our spiritual senses operating effectively is the key to fulfilling our purposes in God's Kingdom.

Developing Your Spiritual Senses

God created humans with five physical senses and designed them to be able to see, smell, hear, feel and taste. Our spirit man has been similarly equipped with five spiritual senses.

But strong meat belongeth to them that are of full age, even those who by reason of use have their senses exercised to discern both good and evil.

—HEBREWS 5:14

Part of activating your gift of discernment will be learning how to exercise your spiritual senses to discern both good and evil. One key to discernment is the importance of identifying which spiritual sense is most predominant in your life.

In the natural, people are more discriminating in some of their senses than others. For example, some people can go into an odiferous place and are completely unaware of the foul smells. Simultaneously, someone with a keen sense of smell might get nauseas from the same odors. Those who have a sensitive and trained ear could pick up a wrong note during a symphony, while their companion might not even realize a wrong note has been sounded. There are an endless number of examples describing the varying degrees of sensory acuity between different individuals.

It is important to keep in mind there are also comparable differences between individuals' sensory acuity in the spirit realm. Do not expect to see in the spirit like someone else. Do not compare your abilities with others, or you will find yourself tricked by our enemy into believing lies. The Word is very clear about not comparing ourselves with others.

For we dare not make ourselves of the number, or compare ourselves with some that commend themselves: but they measuring themselves by themselves, and comparing themselves among themselves, are not wise.

—2 CORINTHIANS 10:12

When God activates the gift of discernment in your life, you will have to discover which spiritual senses are predominant. If for some reason you do not see anything in the spirit, do not panic. Your strength in discerning may be feeling or perceiving things. If that is the case, then allow the Holy Spirit to hone that spiritual sense.

In the next several sections, we will discuss how the five spiritual senses can be utilized. Please understand that these are very brief descriptions and much more could be said and learned about our spiritual senses and our discernment. This is simply providing a foundation to launch forward in practicing your discernment.

Our natural senses are necessary for our existence. Repeatedly our senses protect us from potential hazards. They also allow us to enjoy the beauty of God's creation. As we go through each physical sense and then the corresponding spiritual sense, please keep in mind how interconnected each sense is to our intimacy with the Lord. It would be wrong for you to read this book and think that because now you have a greater head-knowledge of the topic, you also have a greater ability to detect the enemy, or for that matter God's Kingdom and His angels. The point of this book is to create a hunger in you to seek the Lord. Our prayer is that as a result of reading this book, you would ask and allow the Lord to develop the gift of discernment in you to such an extent that you would be able to discern the nuances of His glorious presence. Our Heavenly Father wants to reveal Himself to you in ways beyond description.

A Life of Intercession

This is a small sampling of the potential of what can be discovered. As you commit your life to intercession, you might begin seeing things as you pray. We encourage you to journal the things you see and pray for the interpretation of them. When necessary, you may want to share with your pastor or leaders what the Lord has shown. The things that the Lord shows you are never to glorify you, nor are they to be used to promote yourself and gain either power or recognition.

The Lord has led our church to develop various types of presbyteries to handle the interpretation of dreams, visions, and prophetic words. It might be beneficial for you to contact our church to find out more about developing this kind of ministry in your church or fellowship.

What we are discovering is that the Lord is allowing us to see many of the places in heaven[iv] and other areas that are very dear to His heart.

My prayer is that as you continue to read this book, the gift of discernment will be poured out on you. You will begin perceiving things as you commit your life to pray on behalf of the purposes of God. It will amaze you how your training will be accelerated as you put into practice these principles.

[iii] For a further study of this topic, please refer to Pastor Ron Crawford's book, *Overcoming the Spirit of Infirmity.*

[iv] Two books published by Pneumatikos Publishing describe in more detail the significance of many of these heavenly places, both in the heaven of heavens and in the second heavens. We recommend you read, *Heaven*, by Pastor Ron Crawford and *Ministering from our Heavenly Seats* by Pastor Paul David Harrison.

3

To See or Not To See

In both the natural and the spiritual there are five senses. The one we consciously rely on the most is our sense of sight. Our sight can be a double-edged sword. It gives us the ability to judge our position in relation to objects around us, giving us courage to go forward or warning of danger. Eyesight allows us to make decisions about how to engage or avoid the world around us while it is still distant enough for us to react.

Think about crossing a street and seeing an approaching car. Eyesight allows us to judge our timing in waiting or going ahead, thus avoiding the danger. Conversely, our eyes can very easily deceive us. Just consider how real filmmakers can portray many unbelievable movie scenes. This ability to deceive our eyes is the foundation of the movie industry. In fact, one of the most lucrative sales areas for Hollywood is the "behind the scenes" documentaries that show just how easy it is to fool our eyes.

In the spirit realm, a high percentage of people cannot see. This is a safeguard from the Lord. Those who do see prolifically must be totally submitted to the Lord and grounded in His Word or they will be deceived. The Lord is gracious to open our eyes to see, but it is usually for short periods of time or quick "snapshots".

Without the balancing effect of the other spiritual senses, sight alone is dangerous. Nevertheless, God wants to be able to trust His children to see; knowing that everything we see now, no matter how small or how immense is still seen through a dark glass. It is still seen without the benefit of full light and understanding.

> *For now we see through a glass, darkly; but then face to face:*
> *now I know in part; but then shall I know even as also I am*
> *known.*   —*1 CORINTHIANS 13:12*

Sight

Most of us take our eyesight for granted. What would it be like if we were never able to see the ones we love so dearly? Our eyes allow us to see the stages of our children's growth and enjoy the beautiful earth that God has created.

Can you remember the last time you went into a grocery store to pick out some fruit? Unless you simply did not care, you probably took a close look at the fruit to make sure there were not any blemishes or bruises on it. Likewise, when you are shopping for clothes, you count on your own eyes or those of some trusted friend to help you match colors and styles. Although, judging from the way some people dress, you may wonder if they were blindfolded when they picked out their clothing.

These are insignificant ways in which we use our eyes. Without sight, accomplishing many daily tasks becomes impossible. Consider the limitation and dependencies created by blindness: the inability to drive a vehicle, rescue someone from imminent danger, or identify the source of distant sounds. These are only a few of the ways in which the lack of sight would limit our lives.

If our physical sight is so crucial in our everyday lives, how much more should we value our ability to see in the spirit? Most believers need to have their spiritual eyes opened. If you do not see things in the spirit, you should be praying that God would open your eyes. We are in the midst of the most incredible revelation of the Kingdom of God. The heavens are being opened, and the Lord is sending His angels with gifts and anointings for the body of Christ. The church is in desperate need of these blessings, but if we cannot see into the spirit realm, many of these gifts go unclaimed.

Colors

For example, colors are often depicted in the spirit realm. We need to discern the colors that are predominant on a person or that are apparent in a service. Often there is a particular color surrounding or upon a person to whom we are ministering. The colors on an individual are often associated with a particular gifting that is present in that person. This can be a valuable tool when prophesying to someone or counseling them about their calling.

Each of the colors in the rainbow has meaning and represents one of the Seven Spirits of God that are mentioned several times in Revelation and described individually in other passages of scripture. The Seven Spirits of God represent the way God is currently moving in a situation or with an individual.

*And I beheld, and, lo, in the midst of the throne and of the four beasts, and in the midst of the elders, stood a Lamb as it had been slain, having seven horns and seven eyes, which are **the seven Spirits of God** sent forth into all the earth.*
—REVELATION 5:6

Perceiving colors in the spirit helps us immensely in a ministry setting. For example, if you observe that all the colors of the rainbow are present in a church except indigo blue, you might conclude that particular church is suffering from the Ephesian syndrome. They had everything a church could want, but they had lost their first love, or the presence of the Father (see *Seers Catalog* p.75).

There may be a time when a person seems to have little or no color. This may indicate that the individual lacks an ongoing relationship with the Lord. Black lines and spots also have meaning. Black lines can indicate that the enemy has infiltrated or positioned himself upon a line of unresolved iniquity in a person or congregation. Spots help identify a double agent or an individual that has been sent as an agent of unrighteousness to infiltrate your church (see *Seers Catalog* p.76).

*These are **spots** in your feasts of charity, when they feast with you, feeding themselves without fear: clouds they are without water, carried about of winds; trees whose fruit withereth, without fruit, twice dead, plucked up by the roots;*
—JUDE 1:12

Sometimes the Lord will manifest His colors when we are praying over a world map. He may show certain colors over nations or cities. If the color is dull or lacks vibrancy it may indicate what we need to pray for over that nation. If a nation is fiery red, there may be judgment coming. Obviously, this is not an exact science. There are no formulas to the ways of God. God will teach us, little by little, how to operate with His Seven Spirits often through revealing their predominant color (see *Seers Catalog* p.78). However, colors do indicate a key source of discernment information from God.

Colors also enable us to discern something about the angels that the Lord (or the enemy) sends to us. The Bible contains a wealth of information about the colors associated with various spiritual interactions and we can identify many patterns from its pages. However, God and His Kingdom are so vast and so unexplored that we can only share what we have come to understand. In the ages of eternity, we will look back and laugh at our feeble attempts to describe Him and His Kingdom. We are not trying to teach for facts, those things that we can only base on our experiences, no matter how extensive that experience is. Having said all this, the following descriptions are based on the collective experience of our church body and of many of the saints with whom the Lord has connected us around the world.

Gabriel and his corps of angels leave a rainbow trail of light as they pass through. The angels of the Lord are usually clothed in brilliant white, radiating the presence and glory of God. The Judah angels are generally arrayed in clothing with a white base, accented with bright gold and orange. Michael's contingencies of warring angels usually appear in white based clothes with gold insignias on their shoulders and upper arms. They also have dark, dark blue imbedded stripes across their chests. Fallen angels, on the other hand, exhibit a dingy and faded color because of the absence of the presence of God. However, even given this usual coloring, there are times when a fallen angel will be dressed very similar to an angel of the Lord, appearing as an angel of light (see *Seers Catalog* p. 80).

Perceiving in the spirit will seem strange at times. This is because we are interacting with an invisible world. We are accustomed and comfortable with verifying our perceptions according to the realities of the natural realm. The analytical religious minds of this world contend that one must have solid, verifiable proof in the natural or material realm before they will believe. However, the Lord would have us trust our discernment more than what we see in the natural. The Lord proves Himself and the reality of the spiritual realm through our spirits, not through our flesh. Remember, we walk by faith, not by sight (2 Corinthians 5:7).

Jesus told us not to judge according to our sight or the appearance of something. We are to be like Jesus, and God says that Jesus did not use natural sight to judge or discern. Instead He sought

God the Father for supernatural understanding into His ways. Jesus judged based on that spiritual understanding, not on what He saw or heard in the natural realm.

Judge not according to the appearance, but judge righteous judgment. —JOHN 7:24

And shall make him of quick understanding in the fear of the Lord: and he shall not judge after the sight of his eyes, neither reprove after the hearing of his ears:
—ISAIAH 11:3

Colors can be observed on people, objects, and structures or even on the land. It is very powerful to have an understanding of what colors signify on people. Whether or not you see these colors, spots, lines or clouds on people, they are there. The enemy sees them and because he knows the ways of God, he uses his knowledge of these spiritual indicators to try and hinder God's purposes from being fulfilled in people. Even infants have coloring which represents their purpose and calling in the Lord.

This book can only briefly outline the many lessons we have learned about what colors indicate. For a fuller understanding, we encourage you to secure a copy of Pastor Ron Crawford's book, *Seers Catalog* as a resource for gaining a greater understanding of the colors. He is a gifted seer and Bible scholar. Much of the information in the following sections came out of conversations with Pastor Ron Crawford around specific incidents with which we have been involved. Perhaps this will assist you in learning to interpret what the Lord may show you.

First of all, the most unusual colors are found on those who are closest to the Lord.

Red: This color normally represents a warrior. The person typically has an anointing to propel himself and others into battle on behalf of the purpose of the Lord. It is quite common for this color to be prominent upon someone who moves mightily in the office of the evangelist. It could also represent an anointing that a person has for delivering a knock out punch in the spirit. **As a rule, it would indicate that a person has an anointing to move in a very powerful way in the Spirit of Judgment and Burning** (Isaiah 4:4, 28:6). Many times the color red indicates a suddenly response. It is very important to respond quickly or the perfect timing of the Lord could be missed. This color represents "breakthrough" and a person needs to move

41

immediately when they hear that this color is abiding on them. When you see the color of red flickering, somewhat like a strobe effect, it could mean that there is a point of change taking place or about to take place.

Orange: This vibrant color addresses the importance of people stepping into what they are supposed to be. When you observe this color on someone, it could indicate that God has marked them for advancement or promotion. This color could also point toward the Lord establishing a person in a higher calling within the group or church in which they are a part. However, most often when you see this color on someone, it indicates that they have a gifting of grace to lift up those within the body of Christ. **This anointing of the Spirit of Grace and Supplication is most often released to bless the corporate body or someone else, not the person upon whom it is resting** (Zechariah 12:10, Hebrews 10:29). The person who has this color upon them must be careful to not fall into the trap of thinking they need to be promoted. Frequently this color is seen as a trim color upon someone.

Yellow: When this color is seen upon someone, it is very likely this person has the propensity to move in visions and dreams. **Yellow is the color of the Spirit of Wisdom and Revelation which represents instruction, communication, mystery and, of course, revelation** (Exodus 28:3, Deuteronomy 34:9, Ephesians 1:17). If you see yellow with a white burst, this could indicate that the message is a revelation of Heaven or God's timing. The Oracle in Heaven, which is also known as the *Chronos* area, is most often yellow or gold, although it is sometimes depicted as blue or purple as well. Frequently, those gifted as teacher/seers will have this color of anointing upon them. When a person is speaking and you see a flashing yellow upon them, it could very well indicate that the message they are presenting is a warning from the Lord.

Green: While green represents the Spirit of Prophecy, Life, Supply and Healing (Rev. 8:2, 11:11, 19:10), it can also help identify those with intercessory, prophetic and pastoral giftings. Much like a medicine, the person with green upon them is like a balm (balm of Gilead) for others. When we die to self or are even martyred in the natural, our death literally brings spiritual life to others. Remember, the testimony or *martus* of Jesus is the Spirit of Prophecy (Revelation 19:10). Jesus is the good shepherd or *pastor,* who lays down his life for his sheep.

Light Blue: This sky blue color depicts the Spirit of **Holiness or Saintliness** (Romans 1:4). It presents the picture of a person who has a very pure heart, who is sincere and without guile. This individual has no agenda, is very tenderhearted, and very agreeable. Usually, this color is on people who are called to lead others into saintliness. This color indicates a very holy calling. Many people have this color on them when they first come to know the Lord. Sadly, the color often slowly dissipates as they grow cold in their passion for the Lord and become more "religious".

Indigo Blue: Indigo blue is not usually seen on people. However, when this color does rest upon a person, it usually indicates that they are absorbed in the Lord, and are often so lost in His presence that they totally lose track of time. **Indigo blue represents the Spirit of Glory and of God** (1 Peter 4:14). This deep blue color of the night sky is spoken of when David said, "*the heavens declare the glory of God*" (Psalms 19:1).

Purple: Typically, when you see this color on a person it would indicate that they have real authority to act on behalf of the Lord on an ongoing basis versus a temporary basis. **Purple represents a kingly anointing and speaks of the Spirit of Truth and Sonship** (John 14:17, 15:26, 16:13, Romans 8:15, Galatians 4:6, 1 John 4:6). To see this color would indicate someone who is truly operating in the fullness of God's purpose for their life. Like Jesus, someone who is about His Father's business.

Combinations of Colors: There are probably endless possibilities when you start considering the combinations of colors and anointings. For example, orange and red normally indicate the release of grace and miracles, while green and orange could be a sign that there is a birthing or progressing of the purpose of the Lord. Finally, a rapid changing of colors (kaleidoscope effect) denotes a person who probably can look into a situation and know what is going on. The challenge for a person with this type of anointing is that they may have a tendency to be undisciplined.

The important thing is not for us to create an exhaustive encyclopedia of all possible combinations and interpretations, but for you to learn what to do with the perceptions you receive in the spirit. Pray and seek the Holy Spirit's guidance and that God will give you understanding, realizing there is significance in what you perceive. We must always remain humble, willing and expecting God to change our minds and our hearts. The things that God shows us so often mean we have to give up one more of our preconceived ideas or pet beliefs.

Mantles and Other Accoutrements

Besides seeing colors on a person, the Lord may also reveal unique spiritual vestments. These special spiritual garments are mentioned throughout scripture.

"God gives a mantle to people in the same fashion as He endues a group with a banner. Persons that are moving in power and might before God are covered by individual mantles, insignias or sashes that adorn the garment of white. These serve to identify the measure of authority and calling on behalf of the mission before God". (Seers II, p. 49)

Mantles: In the natural a mantle is a robe, cape, veil, or loose-fitting tunic worn as an outer garment. Many of the prophets wore them (1 Samuel 15:27; 1 Kings 19:13), as did priests (Exodus 28:4) and kings (1 Chronicles 15:27). However, in many cases the scriptures speak of spiritual mantles given to those that are close to the Lord and those with whom He is pleased. It is very much like the Lord is giving a part of Himself to His servants. Mantles can be a sign of promotion and greater authority. Mantles represent the callings, anointings, authority and power that God has vested in His servants.

There are several words used to describe mantles in the Bible. The English words include mantle, coat, and robe. The following verses tell of some of these spiritual mantles.

Elisha knew that it was essential for him to acquire Elijah's mantle if he were to successfully accomplish his prophetic mission. Although Elijah had a physical mantle, it was the spiritual authority that was represented by this mantle that Elisha desired.

*So he departed thence, and found Elisha the son of Shaphat, who was plowing with twelve yoke of oxen before him, and he with the twelfth: and Elijah passed by him, and cast his **mantle** upon him.* —1 KINGS 19:19

*He took up also the **mantle** of Elijah that fell from him, and went back, and stood by the bank of Jordan;* [14]*And <u>he took the **mantle** of Elijah that fell from him, and smote the waters,</u> and said, Where is the Lord God of Elijah? and when he also had smitten the waters, they parted hither and thither: and Elisha went over.* —2 KINGS 2:13-14

Isaiah says the Lord put a special mantle on him. This verse speaks of Isaiah himself, but it also speaks prophetically of the bride of Christ.

I will greatly rejoice in the Lord, my soul shall be joyful in my God; for he hath clothed me with the garments of salvation, <u>he hath covered me with the robe of righteousness,</u> as a bridegroom decketh himself with ornaments, and as a bride adorneth herself with her jewels.

—ISAIAH 61:10

Zechariah records a mighty encounter that Joshua, the high priest, had in heaven. The main focus of this encounter was God clothing Joshua with spiritual garments.

*And he answered and spake unto those that stood before him, saying, Take away the filthy garments from him. And unto him he said, Behold, I have caused thine iniquity to pass from thee, and I will clothe thee with change of **raiment**. ⁵And I said, Let them set a fair mitre upon his head. So they set a fair mitre upon his head, and **<u>clothed</u>** him with garments. And the angel of the Lord stood by.   —ZECHARIAH 3:4-5*

In the New Testament, we are taught that the saints will reign as kings and priests. They will also be clothed with special robes.

*But ye are a chosen generation, a royal **priesthood**, an holy nation, a peculiar people; that ye should shew forth the praises of him who hath called you out of darkness into his marvellous light: —1 PETER 2:9*

We are called to be priests and kings of a holy or saintly nation. The saints are adorned with spiritual garments that have been placed upon them by their Heavenly Father. When we see one another in the spirit or in the heavens, we are dressed according to the giftings and callings that God has put upon us.

The word "clothed" in Hebrew is *labash*. It means to clothe, array, to put upon or wear. This word is very similar to the Greek word used in Luke for "endued".

*And, behold, I send the promise of my Father upon you: but tarry ye in the city of Jerusalem, until ye be **endued** with power from on high.* —LUKE 24:49

This word "endued" also means to clothe, array, have put on, but it also means to invest with clothing. We believe the Lord wants to invest His authority and power by clothing us with heavenly garments.

For in this we groan, earnestly <u>desiring to be clothed upon with our house which is from heaven:</u> [3]If so be that being clothed we shall not be found naked. [4]For we that are in this tabernacle do groan, being burdened: not for that we would be unclothed, but clothed upon, that mortality might be swallowed up of life. —2 CORINTHIANS 5:2-4

On several occasions in the book of Revelation, the Spirit of the Lord refers specifically to the clothing of the saints.

*Thou hast a few names even in Sardis which have not defiled their **garments**; and they shall walk with me in white: for they are worthy. [5]<u>He that overcometh, the same shall be clothed in **white raiment**</u>; and I will not blot out his name out of the book of life, but I will confess his name before my Father, and before his angels.* —REVELATION 3:4-5

And to her was granted that she should be arrayed in fine linen, clean and white: for the fine linen is the righteousness of saints. —REVELATION 19:8

It is very intriguing that just the touch of Jesus' garments had the potency to heal the sick. Could it be the people were actually touching the spiritual garments of the Lord?

*For she said within herself, If I may but touch his **garment**, I shall be whole.* —MATTHEW 9:21

*And besought him that they might only touch the hem of his **garment**: and as many as touched were made perfectly whole.* —MATTHEW 14:36

*And was transfigured before them: and his face did shine as the sun, and his **raiment** was white as the light.* —MATTHEW 17:2

*And his **raiment** became shining, exceeding white as snow; so as no fuller on earth can white them.*

—*MARK 9:3*

Sashes: Sashes are seen in many different colors and tend to be more permanent than mantles. They might take the form of a banner and usually relate to the purpose of a person or group. It may possibly be a sign of empowerment for a particular situation or it could be a more permanent level of authority. When a sash is located across the chest, it usually means it is for a task and will probably be temporary. If the sash is running up and down, it usually identifies authority and is probably more permanent in nature.

Enemies of Righteousness: Fallen angels have mantles and sashes that were given to them by God before the rebellion. For instance, Beelzebub will often be seen dressed as the evil one that he is. However, he will occasionally show himself in his original pre-rebellion attire. Remember, the giftings and callings of God are without repentance. This is how fallen angels manifest themselves as angels of light. We must not be shocked when we see individuals through our spiritual eyes who are not even saved, yet have on spiritual vestments. It is an indication that the enemy either empowers these gifts or has tapped into and twisted the God-given gifts of the individual. Some of the clothing of the enemies of righteousness can be very colorful. It is imperative that we stay so close to the Lord that His light can shine through us to expose these counterfeits.

Beware of false prophets, <u>which come to you in sheep's clothing</u>, but inwardly they are ravening wolves.

—*MATTHEW 7:15*

"The enemy, his operatives and the strongholds that are controlled by the realm of darkness are very much marked and endued with banners and coverings. They are easily identified by color and by combinations of color. Sometimes an insignia or particular marking will offer a telltale sign as to what is operative within that which is seen.

We must be careful in our interpretation, as the brilliance of the hue does not always indicate the veracity or allegiance of the bearer of the standard. A pale or soiled coloring on a spirit being is always a mark of the demonic. Brilliant shades and depictions could be an angel, but it also

47

could be an angel of light that is endued with a higher measure of anointing or authority.

At times we will encounter godly people who appear to be pale or soiled in their coloring, and that could offer a wide array of possibility. It could well be that they are simply depleted due to warfare that has wearied them, drained because of a lack of prayer or it might be due to a mode of enemy infiltration against their devotion to godly purpose." *(Seers II, p.45)*

Keys: The Lord has called us to take dominion and occupy the earth until He returns. The saints are being trained to accomplish this monumental task. One of the accoutrements often seen is a key or set of keys.

*And I will give unto thee the **keys** of the kingdom of heaven: and whatsoever thou shalt bind on earth shall be bound in heaven: and whatsoever thou shalt loose on earth shall be loosed in heaven.* *—MATTHEW 16:19*

Historically, keys represented authority and were positioned on the shoulders or upper body. They usually appear from the forearm down to the hand. They do not look like a key we would be familiar with. The key normally shines with the brightness of one of the Seven Spirits.

*And the **key** of the house of David will I lay upon his shoulder; so he shall open, and none shall shut; and he shall shut, and none shall open.* *—ISAIAH 22:22*

*And to the angel of the church in Philadelphia write; These things saith he that is holy, he that is true, he that hath the **key** of David, he that openeth, and no man shutteth; and shutteth, and no man openeth;* *—REVELATION 3:7*

Shutting and opening are real issues in the spirit realm. God desires that we begin to exercise authority in the causeways of the Spirit, disallowing the things that the enemy has done and allowing what God has ordained. We are called to employ this maneuver in regions, in dimensions, in doorways and spiritual corridors". (Seers II, p. 59-60)

The church has been called to take the battle to the gates. Sometimes these keys actually open up gates and places in the spirit realm. It has been said that whoever controls the watchtower controls the harvest fields. One of the functions of a watchtower was to guard the gates of the city. To enter many of these spiritual gates requires a key. The keys represent the authority the Lord has entrusted to His servants.

There are times that a prophetic word spoken in a timely fashion becomes a key that is able to unlock and enter corridors. Supernatural knowledge and fresh revelation are central ingredients of these prophetic words. Often keys will enable us to get through enemy attacks and territory into which the Lord leads us. The important thing to understand is that the keys are a demonstration of the authority of God placed upon us, not just a medal for us to wear.

Atmospheres

Dark Clouds: Sometimes a "brown out" occurs over a person or place, such as when a dark cloud or eclipse covers the sun. This atmospheric condition usually indicates that a person is being cut off from how they are supposed to be functioning in the spirit. A dark cloud could also be an indication that there is some kind of internal soulish battle taking place in the individual's life. The battle is not necessarily caused by the enemy, but it could be. A dark cloud could represent an ungodly sorrow or even when a person is under pressure from an overbearing spouse who wants to control the relationship.

*And it came between the camp of the Egyptians and the camp of Israel; and it was a **cloud and darkness** to them, but it gave light by night to these: so that the one came not near the other all the night.*   *—EXODUS 14:20*

The cloud that was positioned between the Egyptians and the Israelites appeared dark to the Egyptians. The coloring of the clouds illustrated the difference between those that were moving in the purposes of God and those that were opposed to it. When we observe a dark cloud in a service or on an individual, we should really ask the Lord to show us what specific demonic force is coming against God's purposes and what our response should be.

*And thou sayest, How doth God know? can he **judge through the dark cloud?***   *—JOB 22:13*

49

*Also can any understand the spreadings of the clouds, or the noise of his tabernacle? ³⁰Behold, he spreadeth his light upon it, and covereth the bottom of the sea. ³¹For by them **judgeth he the people**; he giveth meat in abundance. ³²With clouds he covereth the light; and commandeth it not to shine by the **cloud that cometh betwixt**.*

—JOB 36:29-32

Whirlwinds: There are certain times when the moving of the Spirit of the Lord is manifested by whirlwinds.

As for the wheels, it was cried unto them in my hearing, O wheel.   *—EZEKIEL 10:13*

And the cherubims lifted up their wings, and mounted up from the earth in my sight: when they went out, the wheels also were beside them, and every one stood at the door of the east gate of the Lord's house; and the glory of the God of Israel was over them above.   *—EZEKIEL 10:19*

Ezekiel said he saw the Lord being carried on the shoulders of the cherubim. He observed the wheel within a wheel effect. In this passage, the Hebrew word for "wheel" is also translated "whirlwind" in other Old Testament passages. The wheels that Ezekiel was describing had the appearance of a whirlwind. God spoke to Job from out of the whirlwind (Job 38:1). At times, the Lord will reveal Himself to those that are very dear to Him through a whirlwind.

These whirlwinds can manifest in services where the Lord wants to reveal Himself to His people in a more intimate way. These whirlwinds move much like they do in the natural. They can move side to side and up and down. They can also seemingly stay in one position for an extended time.

*Deep calleth unto deep at the noise of thy **waterspouts**: all thy waves and thy billows are gone over me.*

—PSALM 42:7

When you see these whirlwinds manifesting during a service or around an individual, it could very well mean the Lord is drawing them toward the very depths of His heart. If you are in ministry and see a whirlwind, the Lord might have you lead the people to respond to Him in some fashion.

Depending on what the Spirit is trying to accomplish, the whirlwind could speak about other things as well. The whirlwind might be signaling that the church or person is being called to a higher place in God and the work of His Kingdom. God never wants us to get too comfortable with where we are in Him. The Lord is continuously calling us higher.

The Lord loves to use His whirlwind in many different settings. One morning during Sunday School, a young lady who is on the worship team had a gold whirlwind twirling above her head. Our Senior Pastor recognized immediately that the Lord was giving her a new song for the service that day. In order to know how you are to respond to this kind of visitation, you must be able to perceive what is happening and know the voice of the Lord.

It is not uncommon for whirlwinds to be around us as we intercede. Whirlwinds of light may move around us as we pray along with the Lord Jesus Christ on behalf of the purposes of our Heavenly Father. These same kinds of whirlwinds often descend on us as we pray and intercede with one another.

As with so many wonderful things that God does, the enemy will try to move in similar fashion. The enemy has been known to move in the whirlwind, too. When Jesus was with His disciples crossing to the other side of the lake, a great storm rose up and placed them all in great peril. The Greek word used for "storm" in the following verse is referring to a whirlwind.

*But as they sailed he fell asleep: and there came down a **storm** of wind on the lake; and they were filled with water, and were in jeopardy.*   —LUKE 8:23

51

4

Spiritual Sensitivity

Perceiving takes all five of our senses. We have discussed the sense of sight in the previous chapter. However, one sense alone does not bring full perception. The other four senses, both in the natural and in the spiritual, are critical to add the balance, depth and validity to our perceptions.

The truly perceptive individual uses all of their senses to glean a full and true picture of what is occurring around them. To see something beautiful but smell a foul odor should set off warning signals. To feel warmth but taste bile should cause you to consider the discrepancy of your perceptions.

In this chapter, we will explore the four supporting senses, beginning with the most prevalent sense, which is hearing.

Hearing

Many of you have participated in bands or orchestras during your school years. Our band directors had a keen ear for knowing when an instrument was out of tune. Along those same lines, many of us are able to hear our own child's voice out of a group of children. In the spirit, we must learn to distinguish between a person who is crying out in the soulish realm and one who is demonically possessed. We must learn how to differentiate between the voice of an angel of the Lord and the voice of a fallen angel. God wants us to know the difference between the voices of the Father, the Son and the Holy Spirit as well.

53

And thine ears shall hear a word behind thee, saying, This is the way, walk ye in it, when ye turn to the right hand, and when ye turn to the left. —*ISAIAH 30:21*

He that hath an ear, let him hear what the Spirit saith unto the churches. —*REVELATION 3:22*

Listen to Your Divers Tongues

Beyond empowering our intercession, the Lord wants to use the gift of divers tongues to teach us to hear even more things in the spirit realm. If you are not operating in divers tongues, you need to be seeking this powerful gift. We must be careful to not put our prayer times on automatic pilot and remember that what we are speaking forth in tongues is very crucial. Frequently, the sounds we make let us know when and which angels have arrived. For instance, Judah angels bring an anointing of jubilant shouts and horn-like sounds that are accompanied by some of the most extraordinary and excited expressions.

It is utterly astonishing how much you can discern about your location in the spirit realm by simply listening to your divers tongues. There are many times when you will be praying in tongues and suddenly you are saying, "holy, holy, holy". At times, this is the only word that will come out of your mouth. When this happens, there is a strong possibility that you are in the Throne area in heaven. Isaiah was caught up before the Throne and personally witnessed the activity that was going on there. He clearly heard the angels shouting out, "holy, holy, holy".

*And one cried unto another, and said, **Holy, holy, holy**, is the Lord of hosts: the whole earth is full of his glory.*
—*ISAIAH 6:3*

One of the other peculiar things that could happen with your tongues is that they could sound like they are in slow motion. The mystery angels who attend the Oracle[v] speak in this manner. It is not that the angels are speaking slowly, but that the faster they speak the slower it sounds. We have learned that the angels speak at a tremendously quicker rate than we do. This slow motion effect is like the visual effect of a spinning wheel. Although the wheel is actually turning very fast, it appears to be going backward slowly.

You must bear in mind as an intercessor that when you hear these tongues, you need to step fully into the knowledge that you are in these places in heaven. As you do this, you will begin to discern even more about these places. You will also become more aware of your spirit being drawn into these realms in a more compelling way.

It is astounding how many times you will suddenly begin to understand what you are praying when you are praying in the spirit. The Word is very clear that we should pray for the interpretation. We try to always have pen and paper when going into a prayer time to record anything the Lord says or any interpretation He may give.

Supernatural Sounds

Several years ago during a mid-week service, the Lord allowed everyone in our congregation to hear something remarkable in the spirit. We were all listening attentively while our Pastor was teaching when suddenly we heard a *shofar* (Jewish trumpet) sound. Upon hearing the sound, our Pastor asked the congregation if they had heard the sound. Suddenly we all realized the sound was supernatural. There was no natural source of the sound. We all immediately fell on our faces before the Lord and began to pray, knowing the Lord was in our midst.

The next day our Boys Program leader, who had been teaching our boys in another area of the building, asked about the trumpet sound. He and the boys were going up the stairwell near the sanctuary the night before and heard a trumpet blast coming from the sanctuary. They had wondered what visitor was in the service playing the trumpet.

On numerous occasions there have been additional instruments and voices heard during our worship times that were not physically in our service. Sometimes everyone hears them, sometimes only a few. Now and then the Lord desires to open up the ears of different individuals. Allowing them to experience a greater fullness of what is happening in the spirit realm during the worship time.

Encouraging Voices

During prayer, angels sometimes come to convey messages from the Lord. Once in a while, during prayer, angels have come with instructions to turn to a specific passage of scripture through which the Lord wants to speak.

There have been times when the angels have come with instructions to perform a prophetic act on behalf of the Lord. Often when traveling on ministry trips, the Lord will send His angels to welcome us into the area where we have been sent. Once while flying to a city in the northeast part of our country, an angel came and began talking. He was incredibly excited by this visit to the area over which he was watching. His presence was so strong and full of joy that it affected the whole weekend. He spoke of the protection the Lord was providing and the mighty things the Lord was going to accomplish that weekend.

The Lord is so wonderfully faithful. On a ministry trip to India immediately prior to this trip to the northeast, there had been some very intense oppression and discouragement. This angelic visitation brought the needed strength and revitalization for continued ministry.

Discouraging Voices

Unfortunately, there are also voices in the spirit realm that you probably would just as soon not hear. The enemy loves to speak things into our lives. As Christians, we often overlook the fact that the enemy can speak evil *rhema* words to us.

*Blessed are ye, when men shall revile you, and persecute you, and shall say all manner of **evil** (rhema) against you falsely, for my sake.* —MATTHEW 5:11

The tragic thing is that most of us hear more clearly and take to heart more earnestly the words the enemy says, instead of remembering what the Word of God says. The enemy constantly tells us that we are not being used the way we should be or that we are not needed or appreciated. The enemy will tell us lies in order to put us at odds with our brothers and sisters in Christ and especially our leaders.

One of the enemy's favorite places to speak to people is in church. We regularly hear the enemy shouting into our services. He will say that the worship time is too long or the music is too loud. He will say that what is being preached or taught does not make any sense. He will even tell people that they should just leave the service. The enemy loves to tell people that they are being overlooked by the leadership for positions of ministry in the church. Numerous people in our church regularly hear these same things. The enemy uses these same tactics in many churches, but often the people do not recognize what is going on. They do not recognize the enemy's voice, and like the children in the story of the Pied Piper, they just follow the voice without considering its source and intent. The enemy is trying to convince you to give up and not follow the Lord, and he does it in a very deceptive way. Remember, Jesus called him the Father of Lies (John 8:44).

As the Lord opens your spiritual ears, our prayer is that you would hear only His voice. However, the truth is the Lord allows the enemy a certain amount of leeway in this area. Remember Job's comforters? This type of discouraging message from the enemy can wear you out, especially if you do not immediately cast down these thoughts. This constant verbal barrage may be part of what the Spirit meant when He talked about the enemy wearing out the saints.

And he shall speak great words against the most High, and shall wear out the saints of the most High, and think to change times and laws: and they shall be given into his hand until a time and times and the dividing of time.
—DANIEL 7:25

father, let me hear Your Voice

As the Lord increases your ability to hear in the spirit, He will teach you to discern between the voices of our Father, our Lord Jesus Christ and our precious Holy Spirit. This is not always easy to do. For each one of us, the Lord will teach us how to know His voice. This particular kind of training will probably be very personalized.

My sheep hear my voice, and I know them, and they follow me:
—JOHN 10:27

The most important thing we have learned as we have been trained to discern His voice is the wonderful truth that He loves us. One of the Lord's greatest desires is to talk to us. He wants to give you specific prophetic words for your life. The Lord wants us to be more dependent on hearing His voice for ourselves, instead of always being so dependent on outside prophetic voices. Some people are addicted to getting prophetic words and never truly learn how to hear the Lord for themselves.

The Lord desires children who know Him and know His voice. We all need to hear more clearly that still small voice. So often that voice gets bypassed, because we are not patient enough to wait quietly and take the time to tune into its frequency.

Smell

Between the exhaust from overcrowded roadways and the billowing smoke from factories, many big cities are becoming increasingly filled with annoying smells. Therefore, you tend to notice it when you smell something refreshing. For many years, there was a bread factory near our home. The aroma from this factory permeated the surrounding area. Even with your car windows up, the smell of freshly baked bread would make its way into your vehicle. Upon getting in range of this baking bread smell, your stomach would immediately begin growling. The power of the sense of smell would trigger an involuntary reaction from your stomach, and you would begin craving something to eat.

As a young boy I remember making many trips to the grocery store with my mother. I loved to go through the section of the store that displayed fresh fruits and vegetables. One of the best times of the year was when the cantaloupe would come into season. I would want to pick out the biggest ones, but my mom would have to take her time and smell each one. She would pick through them until she found the perfect one that had the sweetest smell.

These are very simple illustrations of the effect our sense of smell can have on our body. As is the case with all our senses, the sense of smell can be developed more fully. Developing your spiritual sense of smell may take some time. Some people are naturally more adept at discerning smells than others. Often it is just a matter of taking the time to discern whether what you smell is in the natural or the spiritual realm.

Your walk with the Lord should be one of constant discovery. We are not talking about the things of the natural realm, but of the spirit. The Lord desires us to focus on His Kingdom and spend less time worrying about the cares of this life. We have decided we want to experience everything we can in the spirit before we leave our earthly bodies to live forever in the presence of the Lord. We want to experience everything God has created for us and prepared for us in His Kingdom.

The Scent of the Lord

One morning when I left the house before Joy and was praying up in the balcony of our church, Jesus came and stood beside me to intercede as He often does. I cannot even recall why I asked the Lord the following question, but I did. I asked Him if I could smell His

58

fragrance. As I lay there feeling His presence, suddenly my nasal passages popped. Very slowly, I began smelling a very sweet, but yet familiar scent. Moment by moment, the scent increased. So much so, that I got up from my normal *proskuneo* (lying down) position to sniff the air.

I walked around the balcony for a few minutes, waiting to see if the aroma would dissipate. I even looked down from the balcony onto the main floor below to see if there was anyone that might be responsible for the unexpected scent. I was surprised to find that I was the only one in the entire sanctuary.

As I continued to walk through the balcony, the scent was growing stronger and stronger. In fact, I had now begun tasting what I smelled. It was simply amazing!

I knew the smell was familiar, but I could not put my finger on it. I finally asked the Lord and He said it was the fragrance of a rose.

I am the rose of Sharon, and the lily of the valleys.
—SONG OF SOLOMON 2:1

This was my first experience of this type. Since that day, I have talked to others who have had similar encounters. One intercessor told me that they had smelled frankincense when the Lord visited them. Your experience may be totally different, and that is part of the beauty of the awesomeness of our God. The important thing is that the Lord wants to activate your spiritual sense of smell.

Who is this that cometh out of the wilderness like pillars of smoke, perfumed with myrrh and frankincense, with all powders of the merchant?
—SONG OF SOLOMON 3:6

Often our sense of smell is a measure of the level of intimacy we have with someone. Typically, I can identify my wife when she is near by the particular fragrances she uses. I want to have such acuity of smell that I can recognize a personal visitation of the Lord. I believe the Lord wants to reveal Himself to all of us in this way. I strongly believe that nothing would please our Lord more than to have His fragrance fill the very places where we worship Him.

What Is That Smell?

Chances are that you will also encounter smells that are produced by the presence of the enemy. During the deliverance of someone, is not uncommon to encounter foul smells as spirits are dispelled from these individuals. However, you could also encounter various kinds of smells at church during intercession or even during the activity of your busy day. The crucial thing is to stay aware of your spiritual surroundings and not be ignorant of the enemy's devices.

Lest Satan should get an advantage of us: for we are not ignorant of his devices. —2 CORINTHIANS 2:11

Unlike Paul's pleasant experience, I often encounter evil, foul odors. Once I was walking along the passage behind our platform when I literally walked into a burning, sulfur-like smell. My first reaction was to search for the source, perhaps a light ballast or wire burning. There was absolutely no physical source. The smell was very localized. I could actually walk in and out of it and did so several times in the course of my investigation. I knew a demonic being had come to disrupt our service, so I found our Senior Pastor and reported what was happening. We prayed for God's protection and wisdom in dealing with whatever strategy the enemy was pursuing against us. A few minutes, later several individuals arrived purposely to disrupt the service. God caused their attempt to utterly fail and they left with their destructive mission unfulfilled.

Several times, one or the other of us have been awakened during the middle of the night by a curious odor. The odors are definitely not from natural sources, nor are they of the Lord. An evil spirit or sometimes a human spirit has astral projected into our room. When this occurs we simply need to seek the Lord. He is our protection and will give the victory.

The enemy is extremely active during the night. He loves to attack us while we are sleeping. We pray before going to bed that the Lord would cover our family and home during the night. The Lord is always watching over us. However, just like the Children of Israel and the story of Job, the Lord will allow the enemy some access to us in order to train us how to withstand and overcome the devices of our enemy. We have asked the Lord to be our teacher and guide. We must believe the Lord and submit to whatever the Lord allows into our lives, because it is for our training.

Now these are the nations which the Lord left, to prove Israel by them, even as many of Israel as had not known all the wars of Canaan; ²Only that the generations of the children of Israel might know, to teach them war, at the least such as before knew nothing thereof;   *—JUDGES 3:1-2*

As we move into the deeper things of the Lord, we will have more encounters with enemy forces. These are opportunities for the Lord to prove or test us. He is teaching us the basics of how to identify, as well as battle, the enemy. So if you are awakened at night by a strange smell, possibly sulfur or rotten eggs, and perceive that the enemy has entered your room, do not fret. Just begin praying in the spirit and find out what God would have you do. It could be you need to pray a prayer of covering before you go to bed or it could be the Lord is allowing the enemy to enter your house for a reason. You will have to seek the Lord to find out His intent in each situation.

Taste

For us, tasting things in the spirit is still a work in progress. It is one area where both of us need further discernment development. Paul told how he tasted the sweetness of the roses when Jesus came and visited him, but beyond that we have no other personal examples to share. However, scripture speaks over and over again about tasting in the spirit realm.

*Is there iniquity in my **tongue**? cannot my **taste** discern perverse things?*   *—JOB 6:30*

*O **taste** and see that the Lord is good: blessed is the man that trusteth in him.*   *—PSALM 34:8*

*How sweet are thy words unto my **taste**! yea, sweeter than honey to my mouth!*   *—PSALM 119:103*

*If so be ye have **tasted** that the Lord is gracious.*   *—1 PETER 2:3*

*And I took the little book out of the angel's hand, and ate it up; and it was **in my mouth sweet** as honey: and as soon as I had eaten it, my belly was bitter.*   *—REVELATION 10:10*

One act of intimacy that we must consider when talking about the sense of taste is kissing. Every believer needs to experience the sweet kiss of the Lord. As you spend more and more time with Jesus, you will discover He is incredibly affectionate.

*Let him **kiss** me with the kisses of his mouth: for thy love is better than wine.*

—SONG OF SOLOMON 1:2

*Thou gavest me no **kiss**: but this woman since the time I came in hath not ceased to kiss my feet.*   *—LUKE 7:45*

Touch

Often when people do not see things in the spirit they get very discouraged. The enemy loves to reinforce these feelings by attacking you with thoughts of falling behind in your giftings. There are many believers who see far more things than we do in the spirit. It is easy to get a little jealous of those who have these visual or auditory giftings, but the other three senses, including the sense of touch, are usually more reliable than seeing and hearing.

Just consider television. Think about all the "behind the scenes" shows that demonstrate how easy it is to fool someone with sight and sound. We quoted the verse earlier in which the Word specifically says Jesus would not use His eyes and ears to discern.

*And shall make him of quick understanding in the fear of the LORD: and he shall not judge after the sight of his **eyes**, neither reprove after the hearing of his **ears**:*

—ISAIAH 11:3

Touched by an Angel

You must learn to trust the Lord. It is completely in His hands if you do or do not see something in the spirit. You cannot force yourself to see in the spirit. The Lord has encouraged us to utilize the giftings He has given. Be faithful in what you have and you will receive more. We both have a greater tendency to sense things in the spirit. You might want to call it "feeling". Although we often do not see angels, we certainly can sense when they are present. My first encounter with an angel was hearing him speak to me, but it was not long before other angels began touching me to let me know that they were with me. It was hard to go home and tell Joy what had happened. I was not sure if I was crazy or not.

Often when angels come, the side of my face will heat up. For others, there may be a tingling or vibration that you sense somewhere on your body. Joy tells me she usually feels a hot hand on her shoulder or on the crown of her head. There may be times when you walk through a group of angels and it will feel like you are walking through an electrical field. To some it may feel like warm water.

I have had angels place their hands on my head, grab my ankles and even hold my hands. When they first started doing this, I would react rather dramatically from the glory of the Lord that radiated from them.

Many times when I am ministering, the Lord or an angel will place something in my hand to give to others. You can feel it in your hand until it has been distributed to everyone who was supposed to receive it. Similarly, I have felt fire come on me. Often when this happens, my hands will get extremely hot and I know that this is an indication that I need to pray for people.

Once I was ministering in Wisconsin, and I felt heat in my right hand. The Lord told me that He was giving me swords to give to the intercessors that were in attendance at the meeting. I touched the right hand of each of the intercessors. Following the service, several trusted seers told me that as I prayed for people they could see the swords appearing in their hands. Some of them had special engravings on them.

Once when we were in Argentina, Pastor Paul and Pastor Crawford went together to pray in the city. While they were gone, I felt led of the Lord to seek Him; soon an angel came and brought me a package. It was like a liquid-filled balloon. I could feel the smoothness of the membrane and the movement of the liquid inside. I asked the angel what it was and what I was supposed to do with it. He told me to just trust the Lord and take it back with me to the USA. He said I would be told what to do with it. Then both the angel and the feeling of the package in my hands faded.

Several weeks later during a Saturday prayer time at our church, one of our members brought a visiting pastor from Mexico. They came and sat in the back of the room. Our Pastor greeted them via a Spanish translator, and suddenly the Lord told me to give this visitor the package I had received in Argentina. The Lord also told me to tell this Mexican pastor there was a gift within the gift for his wife. I was instructed to tell him to lay his hands on his wife when he returned to Mexico and impart the gift to her as well.

As soon as the teaching time was over, I found someone who could translate for me and obeyed the Lord, delivering both the message and the gift from the Lord. Believe me; all of this takes great faith and a willingness to be thought a fool for Christ's sake.

Within a month, a report came back that mighty healing miracles had begun in this dear Mexican Pastor's ministry as soon as he returned from visiting our church. The report also said that his wife, who unbeknownst to us, had been diagnosed with cancer, was now completely whole and seeing healing miracles happen through her prayers as well. Trusting in a touch from the Lord is mighty.

Instead of ignoring the sensations of your body, you should instead begin to pay attention and be prepared for a message from the Lord.

Discerning the Temple of the Holy Spirit

In Pastor Ron Crawford's booklet, *Manual of the Seven Spirits*, he lines up the Seven Spirits with seven specific areas of the body (p. 91).

Location	Color / Spirit of God	Identity and Meaning
Top of the Head	**Violet** Truth, Sonship	Crown of Royalty and Truth
Face	**Indigo Blue** Glory and Presence of God	Face to Face with the Glory of God
Shoulder	**Light Blue** Holiness and Saintliness	Saintly Commission / Rank; Government upon the Shoulders
Upper Torso & Chest	**Green** Life, Supply and Prophecy	Our Identity as a Person and Minister
Lower Torso & Loins	**Yellow** Wisdom and Revelation	Understanding; Strength of Belief; Productivity and Reproduction
Thigh and Knees	**Orange** Grace and Supplication	Promotion and Advancement; Strengthen the Feeble Knees (Climb)
Feet	**Red** Judgment and Burning	Victorious March of Conquest; Soles Tread and Possess

If you are feeling powerful sensations in some specific area of your body, they might possibly indicate a particular Spirit of the Lord is moving at that time.

We almost hate to speak with this level of detail, because invariably some self-seeking individual will try to convince themselves or others that they are experiencing these manifestations of God's touch. They will use our words to glorify themselves or to seek recognition and authority that is not God-given. Knowing this danger, we are writing these things and trusting the Lord to direct them to His humble servants to whom He is desirous of teaching His ways.

To use discernment for either selfish or evil intentions, as with any other gifting of the Lord, is to heap to yourself judgment.

Discernment Activations

One of the assignments we give to help students in our discernment classes stir up their gift of discernment is to send them to a particular place to discern what is going on there in the spirit realm. After the class receives a certain level of instruction on the gift of discerning of spirits, they are asked to go to a specific local bookstore. The Lord identified the bookstore during prayer one day and said that He was going to activate our students' spiritual senses and empower their gift of discernment when they went there for this assignment.

The key lesson in this assignment is how important it is to learn what God does to alert you to the fact that there are demonic forces in an area.

This particular bookstore has a full spectrum of enemy influences. Before our students ever go into the store we have them plead the blood of Jesus upon themselves. As this is an assignment of the Lord, there is no reason for fear in this situation. Each individual walks through the bookstore not paying attention to what section of the bookstore they are in. After they have walked around a few minutes, they sit down at a table and write down what they saw, heard, smelled, tasted or felt in the spirit. They are asked to write down any pain, nausea or other reaction in their body and where it was located.

Next, they walk back through the store, this time taking note of what they sense when they are in certain areas of the bookstore. For instance, are they in the horror section, religious section, mystery or sci-fi section when they sense a certain reaction? They note any unusual physical or spiritual manifestations that may occur when they are in the various sections of the store.

It is absolutely incredible the things that happen as our students have done this assignment. The students have been both teenagers and adults. Almost without exception everyone discerns some kind of physical manifestation of what they are sensing in the spirit realm. Some saw demons as they entered the store. However, the good news is that the Lord sent His angels to give them safe passage during this assignment. Some folks who had never sensed anything in the spirit were immediately gifted to do so. Many people experience same kinds of pains and oppression as other students without ever knowing what others have reported.

Even though we knew this was a place that the enemy uses to market many of his vile books, the Lord has had us continue to use this facility to train people from across the United States and other parts of the world. We believe the Lord is going to take this store and turn it for good, but until then we will continue to use it to train people in utilizing their gift of discernment.

The Lord has His own reasons, but He did specifically teach us to discern the evil before He gave similar assignments to teach us to discern the good. Remember, the scripture says we are to have our senses exercised to discern both good and evil.

But strong meat belongeth to them that are of full age, even *those who by reason of use have their senses exercised to* **_discern both good and evil_**.

—HEBREWS 5:14

In our second course on discernment, the students are placed into teams of four or five and assigned specific areas of our city in order to discern the demonic activity at work in that area. Once again, God is always faithful to show the different teams the strongholds of the enemy in their assigned area. Several saw demons and demonic structures in the spirit realm. One group saw demons disappear into the ground as they drove into the area. We also instruct our students to discern what God's original intent was for that place before it became inhabitant by the spirits that are there.

It is especially critical that we teach our young people to walk in a high level of discernment. We train our little children in a variety of ways, too. Our children need to have their spirits developed to be able to discern the evil influences on television shows, video games, movies, music and websites they encounter.

Most of us use the Internet on a regular basis. Sometimes when you are doing research, you hit a website with which you are not familiar. You would be amazed how the Holy Spirit alerts through discernment that the particular website is evil. Often I will be working away at my computer with Joy fixing dinner in the kitchen and suddenly my chest tightens up and uneasiness settles in. Usually this feeling is so strong that I know something is wrong with the website before I really look at the site at all. Typically, it only takes a few more clicks to see a confirmation of the forewarning from the Spirit.

Overcoming Spiritual Handicaps

In the natural, we speak of those who cannot use all five of their natural senses as being handicapped or disabled. The scriptures say we are all handicapped in the spiritual realm until our earthly bodies are swallowed up by our eternal bodies. We all perceive partially and know partially, looking forward to the day when we will perceive and know perfectly.

For we know in part, and we prophesy in part. [10]But when that which is perfect is come, then that which is in part shall be done away. [12]For now we see through a glass, darkly; but then face to face: now I know in part; but then shall I know even as also I am known.

—1 CORINTHIANS 13:9, 10, 12

Every one of us is handicapped in the spirit. At this juncture in our walk with the Lord, rarely do we see things in the spirit with open vision. There was a time we thought not being able to see in the spirit was a huge shortcoming. However, we have been determined to go on with the Lord, whether we could see in the spirit or not, and the Lord has been gracious to develop many of our other senses. He is teaching us to discern what is going on in the spirit realm through a combination of the other four spiritual senses.

There are many amazing stories about blind people who have overcome their handicap to not only function in society, but to become very proficient in whatever they put their minds to. Whether it is playing a musical instrument or learning how to ride a bicycle, they realize that they want to experience life to the fullest.

As saints, most of us want to experience the Lord in ways we have not known. When the Lord said He wanted to teach us to sense things in the spirit realm with senses other than vision, we had no idea how He would accomplish it. The best way to explain how He did this is to relate it to how a blind person compensates for their lack of eyesight by utilizing their other senses. Many blind people learn how to read with their hands. They also develop extremely sensitive hearing, smelling and touch. They learn to pay attention to their other senses, developing them to a level of ability that people with normal eyesight never accomplish.

God is such a wonderful Father; I love it when He simply calls my name. Often He will say, "Paul, I love you". He often sends His

Holy Spirit to teach me to know His ways better. One lesson I will never forget is when He taught me to use my divers tongues to locate where I was when I was interceding. The beauty of this is that the Lord will sometimes open my eyes to see a glimpse of where I am and then close them again. It is nice to have a confirmation like this, but for the most part the Lord does not give confirmations, as that would defeat His purpose to teach us to live by faith. You must walk in faith.

We mentioned earlier that when you are in the Oracle, your tongues might sound like they are in slow motion. Once you realize that you are in a place such as the Oracle, you just continue to intercede and write down any revelation you get. As you step into believing that you are really there, your spirit will get more immersed into that realm.

As you listen to your divers tongues very intently, you will notice that often your accent will change. Sometimes, this is due to the fact that someone else in the spirit is talking to you. In many ways, our divers tongues operate as radar for incoming sounds and images.

Echolocation

A recent television documentary told the story of a blind man who had learned to ride a bike. He rides bicycles both on busy streets and off-road. His ability to know where cars, trees, poles and other objects are just by the clicking of his tongue was uncanny. The process he used was called echolocation.

Echolocation is defined as a physiological process for locating distant or invisible objects by means of sound waves reflected back to the emitter by the objects. Bats, some whales and other marine mammals use echolocation to find their prey or their way. Echolocation is the use of ultra-high frequency sounds for navigation. In echolocation, a high-pitched sound (usually clicks) is sent out by these creatures. The sound bounces off the object and then returns to the animal. These creatures interpret the returning echo to determine the object's shape, direction, distance, and texture.

The blind bike rider has become so proficient that he has been able to teach other blind people how to utilize this "clicking" sound to navigate their way around their dark world. According to the documentary, it is much easier to teach someone who is completely blind this process than someone who has partial sight.

The Lord is in the business of teaching His children to operate with His Spirit and in the spirit realm. Perhaps the reason so many of us do not see in the spirit is because He wants us to hone our other spiritual senses.

Diverslocation

The Lord began teaching some things through the principles that were used in echolocation. First of all, when a sightless animal clicks, whistles or makes some kind of sound it produces an image from them. This illustrates the importance of using our divers tongues to produce vision for both the church and each of us individually. Bats are able to find an insect the size of a pinhead. The more we use our divers tongues, the more accurate our vision of what the Lord is revealing will become. Divers tongues help release the mysteries and revelations – those things that cannot be seen or understood with the natural mind.

For he that speaketh in an unknown tongue speaketh not unto men, but unto God: for no man understandeth him; howbeit in the spirit he speaketh mysteries.
—*1 CORINTHIANS 14:2*

Secondly, bats make a chirping sound when they are flying. When a bat is gagged it will not even move.

I thank my God, I speak with tongues more than ye all:
—*1 CORINTHIANS 14:18*

This could suggest that if we do not utilize our divers capacity that we could become immovable in our forward spiritual progression. If there is no forward movement, there will be loss of confidence in the Lord and the gifts that He has bestowed upon us. Notice that when there is no movement, there is also no vision or direction.

Where there is no vision, the people perish: but he that keepeth the law, happy is he. —*PROVERBS 29:18*

It is almost like being paralyzed in not moving forward in our God-given purpose in life.

Finally, bats cannot use the sounds from other bats to get their navigational information. We must realize the importance of our individual intercession. We could compare the navigational information that is received by the animals with our ability to interpret our tongues and the things we are sensing when we are praying in tongues.

It is really up to us how limited our experiences in the spirit realm will be. The Lord wants to gift every believer with divers tongues and discernment. We must learn to make use of our divers tongues to their fullest capacity. You can know where you are by listening to your divers tongues. It takes a lot of practice, and it will also take faith, but it can be done.

So many Christians believe that God's gifts always come fully developed, but that is very far from the truth in the natural and very far from the truth in the spirit. Gifts must be developed and exercised to be useful.

The Lord wants to train and equip you. Be open to Him teaching you how to discern using your spiritual senses in the way He wants. Pursue the Lord with all your heart and allow Him to teach you to be able to discern the wonderful things of the spirit realm.

If we could give you any advice in this area, it would be that you can go as far in the Lord as you are willing to pray and commune with Him. Do not allow thoughts of how you are coming behind in some gifting to prevent you from allowing the Lord to teach you more about Himself. He loves you and wants to reveal amazing things about Himself to you.

He teaches His way, and His way is uniquely designed for each of His individual children. It is a custom-built, individual development plan. Be willing to learn whatever lesson He brings your way. Do not be as some foolish ones who want to tell God the best way for them to learn, because they are always wrong and ultimately suffer through the longest, hardest lessons. Before He can teach you how to operate in the giftings He has given to you, He will always teach humility, submission and relationship communing with Him.

---

[v] The oracle is an area of heaven, which is represented in the earthly temple by the Holy of Holies. It is a place where the mysteries of God are kept and from which they are released. For further study, see *Heaven,* by Ron Crawford. (2 Samuel 16:23, 1 Kings 6:19, Psalm 28:2, Hebrews 8:5, 9:1-11, 10:19-25, Ephesians 3:10-12, Romans 16:25-26.)

5

Developing Your Discernment

As with every gifting, one has to grow and mature in it. With the gift of discerning of spirits, continue to ask the Lord to increase your level of discernment on a regular basis. This is not a gift that is fully developed when it is given. It is a gift that grows more powerful with use.

Think about what level you are presently operating at in this gift. For example, are you able to distinguish between what is spirit and what is flesh? Do you know when an evil spirit or human spirit is present? As you mature in your discernment you will be able to discern when there is a sudden change in the spiritual atmosphere. Ideally, you want to be able to discern what the Spirit has come to accomplish.

As you walk in this remarkable gift, you should gradually be able to distinguish between the presence of the Heavenly Father, Jesus Christ our Lord and the Holy Spirit of God, even without seeing them. As saints, we must learn to know when angels arrive and have the ability to communicate with them to find out why they have been sent. You need to learn to differentiate between the various kinds of angels the Lord may send. We have already established that the gift of discerning of spirits is for the identifying both of good and evil (Hebrews 4:12). So finally, you will need to know the difference between a demon and a dark angel. As we proceed, we will discuss each of these areas in greater detail.

73

The Presence of the Heavenly Father

During intercession, each experience that we have with the Father and the things that go on around His Throne can be different. There is a tremendous amount of activity that goes on around the Throne. Your spirit may feel like it is going to explode from within. You may sense such a measure of the holiness of God that you feel like you are going to die. You may even hear the angels and elders crying out holy, holy, holy as you worship before your Father.

And the four beasts had each of them six wings about him; and they were full of eyes within: and they rest not day and night, saying, Holy, holy, holy, Lord God Almighty, which was, and is, and is to come.

—REVELATION 4:8

The voice of the Father is very loving, but very forceful, too. It can be a still small voice and at other times it may thunder throughout your being. Sometimes the way you breathe changes when you are in the presence of the Father. It is very important to write down the details of what happens in you when you are in His presence.

Do not be surprised if you feel a measure of His love that absolutely overwhelms you.

There are places in the Father that He may permit you to experience. He may let you into His heart and allow you to enter the portals that are within it. There are secret places within the Throne where you can worship and be ministered to one-on-one by Him. There is a very real hiding place where the Father can put you.

He that dwelleth in the secret place of the most High shall abide under the shadow of the Almighty.

—PSALM 91:1

There are nuances of His presence that the Father will teach you as you seek and commune with Him. It is during these intimate times with the Lord that He will show you how to distinguish the voice and manifest presence of each person of the Godhead.

Abiding With Jesus

The Lord Jesus Christ manifests Himself in many ways. We already shared with you the smell of one of His fragrances. It is amazing how He continues to reveal Himself as you intercede with Him. Jesus is the chief intercessor and those who would want to know Him in a more intimate way need to intercede with Him.

Who is he that condemneth? It is Christ that died, yea rather, that is risen again, who is even at the right hand of God, who also maketh intercession for us.
—ROMANS 8:34

Wherefore he is able also to save them to the uttermost that come unto God by him, seeing he ever liveth to make intercession for them.   —HEBREWS 7:25

We must learn to discern when He has come to visit us. Jesus will come as you intercede for His Father's purposes. Usually there are reactions within your spirit when He comes. Again it is common to experience a shortness of breath. There is also an overwhelming sense of His love. He is always very encouraging and never condemning. There is such an atmosphere of humility and gentleness that abides upon Him.

These kinds of things can be discerned as you exercise your gift of discernment. The Lord wants you to know and experience Him in fresh ways. He is desirous for you to know Him in an intimate way.

Take my yoke upon you, and <u>*learn of me*</u>*; for I am meek and lowly in heart: and ye shall find rest unto your souls.*
—MATTHEW 11:29

John the Beloved knew this place of intimacy with His Lord. His favorite place was lying right next to the heart of the Lord.

He then lying on Jesus' breast saith unto him, Lord, who is it?
—JOHN 13:25

This kind of intimacy brings about amazing results. First, even though John was the youngest disciple, he was the only one who did not forsake Jesus on the cross. It was through John's close relationship with Jesus that John had the courage to watch as Jesus was crucified.

It was also John who learned the importance of abiding in the Lord. It was through his continual pressing into the Lord that he received such incredible revelations. Through knowing the Lord, John was one to whom Jesus revealed what was going to happen in the last days. The Lord shares very special secrets with His friends.

75

Surely the Lord God will do nothing, but he revealeth his secret unto his servants the prophets.
—*AMOS 3:7*

This is a regular pattern with the Lord. He continues to share those secrets and mysteries with those who would commit to His purposes and be His friends. When we spend time with Jesus, it will be a natural progression for us to find out what the Father wants to accomplish on this earth. Jesus is always about doing His Father's business.

And he said unto them, How is it that ye sought me? wist ye not that I must be about my Father's business?
—*LUKE 2:49*

This is what Jesus was busy doing when He lived here on this earth, and this is what He is busy doing today from Heaven.

Jesus loves to come and minister to us. It is such a blessing to receive visits from Him on a regular basis. He will lay His hands on you and pray for you. It is very real, but it must be discerned. He will hold you and He will even kiss you. Jesus is incredibly affectionate with us. There have been times when He prayed for me and I physically shook for an extended period of time. No one was laying hands on me. In fact, I was all alone in intercession when He came and ministered to me.

The Lord will also come and take you places. He may take you into the second heavens where He is very busy preparing places and making preparations for the battle with Satan and the fallen angels.

In my Father's house are many mansions: if it were not so, I would have told you. I go to prepare a place for you. 3And if I go and prepare a place for you, I will come again, and receive you unto myself; that where I am, there ye may be also.
—*JOHN 14:2-3*

He may take you to places in the Heaven of Heavens, also known as the Third Heaven. He may take you to a chamber where He fellowships with you and shares the plans He has in store for you or your ministry in the future.

During these times of intimacy, most likely you will feel completely alone with Him. You will have His undivided attention. You will be very humbled by the fact that you are receiving such incredible attention from One so high and lifted up. Why would Jesus, who has so much to do, want to spend time with you? He loves you and never tires of being with you. You are the apple of His eye.

> *Keep me as the apple of the eye, hide me under the shadow of thy wings,*   *—PSALM 17:8*

You are always on His mind. He desires and longs to be with you and commune with you. Will you give Him some of your time? Even more importantly, will you be able to know when He has come?

In the Wind of the Holy Spirit of God

The Holy Spirit is much more vast and illusive than we could ever imagine. The Spirit moves when and where He wants. There are facets to the Spirit that God is beginning to reveal to His church so that we can know the ways of the Lord. The ways of God are also the ways of His Spirit. The key is learning what these ways are and how to identify them when they are moving in our lives and when we are ministering.

As we stated earlier, there are actually Seven Spirits of God mentioned in the Word.

> *John to the seven churches which are in Asia: Grace be unto you, and peace, from him which is, and which was, and which is to come; and from the seven Spirits which are before his throne;*   *—REVELATION 1:4*

> *And unto the angel of the church in Sardis write; These things saith he that hath the seven Spirits of God, and the seven stars; I know thy works, that thou hast a name that thou livest, and art dead.*   *—REVELATION 3:1*

> *And out of the throne proceeded lightnings and thunderings and voices: and there were seven lamps of fire burning before the throne, which are the seven Spirits of God.*
> *—REVELATION 4:5*

And I beheld, and, lo, in the midst of the throne and of the four beasts, and in the midst of the elders, stood a Lamb as it had been slain, having seven horns and seven eyes, <u>which are the seven Spirits of God sent forth into all the earth.</u>

—REVELATION 5:6

These Seven Spirits[vi] make up the Spirit of God and characterize how He is moving at a particular time. The most prolific demonstration of the Seven Spirits is in the seven colors that are in the rainbow. These colors can be discerned often in services and on people. It is essential as we move as the sons of God that we develop our ability to know and understand the manifestation of these colors that represent the Spirit of God.

Discernment's Many Uses

The gift of discerning of spirits can be used in business, witnessing, counseling, shopping, at school, at home, to name only a few of the many other places. Basically, discernment is always useful.

In almost any job, we are required to interact with people on a daily basis. We must learn to be more sensitive and listen to what the Spirit may be trying to tell us as we go through our busy day. We must have our discernment exercised so that we can know when we step into a place of business if there are evil spirits at work.

More and more, businesses are becoming fronts for enemy activity. There are many businesses that try to sell you legitimate products and services, but in addition they try to sell you things that are directly from the enemy. Many times the Lord allows us to discern evil spirits working in individuals with whom we are dealing in some kind of business transaction. We are not saying that we should not love these individuals, but we better use discretion in how close of a relationship we are to have with them.

Do you remember the story of the Gibeonites as told in Joshua 9? They saw the power and favor of God on the Children of Israel. They wanted to share in that blessing, so the Gibeonites tricked the Children of Israel into making an alliance. We must always be careful with whom we align and partner.

And when the inhabitants of Gibeon heard what Joshua had done unto Jericho and to Ai, ⁴They did work wilily, . . . ¹⁴And

*the men took of their victuals, and <u>asked not counsel at the</u>
<u>mouth of the LORD</u>. [15]And <u>Joshua made peace with them, and</u>
<u>made a league with them, to let them live: and the princes of</u>
<u>the congregation sware unto them</u>. . . . [22]And Joshua called for
them, and he spake unto them, saying, Wherefore have ye
beguiled us, saying, We are very far from you; when ye dwell
among us? . . . [24]And they answered Joshua, and said, Because
it was certainly told thy servants, how that the LORD thy God
commanded his servant Moses to give you all the land,*
                                            —JOSHUA 9:3-4, 14-15, 22, 24

When witnessing to someone, it is essential that we be able to
discern. Many times the Lord wants to show us what spirits are
coming against individuals. Often the type of spirit that is coming
against them will indicate to us the iniquity that is at the root of their
situation. Then the Lord will give us the power to help them overcome
it. God wants us to learn how to pinpoint areas in people's lives that
have kept them from coming to the knowledge of the truth. Remember
the story of Jesus with the woman at the well, how he told her through
discernment about her life and her situation?

*The woman then left her waterpot, and went her way into the
city, and saith to the men, [29]<u>Come, see a man, which told me</u>
<u>all things that ever I did: is not this the Christ?</u>*
                                            —JOHN 4:28-29

Schools, even Christian schools, are full of all kinds of
demonic influences. Our children need to be gifted in discernment so
that they can know what kind of spirits may be at work in their
classmates. Many times you can sense spirits that have attached
themselves to people who are involved in a sinful situation. Our young
people need to learn to pick up on these kinds of evil spirits so they
will know not to hang around with certain of their classmates.

The enemy is seeking to seduce and ultimately destroy our
young people. How often it is that good young people get themselves
into bad situations because of the kind of friends they have chosen. As
parents, we would love to be able to protect our children from the
enemy's devices. However, our children must mature in the Lord and
learn to discern for themselves.

As far as counseling, it is imperative that you be able to
discern spirits. Many times people walk into the office and the spirits

that have been a part of their lives for many years walk in with them. Sometimes these evils spirits actually waited outside while the individual was being counseled. We must be sensitive to the spiritual atmosphere that is present in our counseling sessions.

Spirits of confusion will try to hinder the communication process. Once during a conversation with someone in my office, an evil spirit actually reached out of the ground and robbed the thoughts of the person talking. They completely forgot what they were talking about. This was not a person with some demonic problem; this was a very gifted leader in our church. We can sometimes be forgetful, but in this case it was not forgetfulness. We must also be aware that the enemy can rob us of our thoughts.

Human spirits can project into a counseling situation, too. These human spirits can cause various distractions depending on their abilities to operate in the spirit realm. We must be careful how we deal with these human spirits. We bless them and speak forth the love of the Father and then send them on their way. You must be sensitive to the possibility of this occurring.

Our homes can be places that the enemy will try to infiltrate. We must guard our homes. We need to plead the blood of Jesus and ask for a fresh sprinkling of His blood upon them. We also need to break off any enemy assignments or word curses.

If problems continue to persist after you have taken these precautions, you may have to ask the Lord to give you either words of knowledge or insights as to what you should do next. At times you may sense evil presences in your home. The first question you must ask is, "Has there been a breach?" Have you, your spouse or your kids brought anything into your home that might give the enemy legal access into your home?

You may want to check the house for videos, CD's, books or any number of things that the enemy uses as a loophole to come in our homes. We need to come into a level of discernment that we could pick up a video or DVD and tell whether there are demonic attachments.

We have known many people with problems which constantly occur in their homes. When they went through the process of discerning the good and evil, they would find the source of their trouble and be able to eliminate it. Sometimes, the problem is that human spirits have been projecting into their homes. When we ask the

Lord to prevent evil spirits from attacking our families and homes, we usually do not think to pray for protection from human spirits. So the enemy will use these ones who are practicing his wicked ways to get around the prayers of protection from the saints of God. Through trial and error, the Lord taught us that we had to pray specifically that human spirits would not be allowed to enter our home. When we prayed this particular prayer, the problem immediately ceased.

You have to be very specific as to how you pray about the humans that astral project. Do not cast or assign these human spirits to hell. These spirits represent people who are alive, but desperately need the Lord. They are hungry for the supernatural but have unwittingly become willing participants in the spiritual deceptions of the enemy. All we need to do is bless them and then send them back to their homes. We often pray that God's presence will be so real to them and that all the lies they have believed will be revealed. Pray that they will know the truth and come to know the God of all truth.

But I say unto you, Love your enemies, bless them that curse you, do good to them that hate you, and pray for them which despitefully use you, and persecute you;
—MATTHEW 5:44

Great fear can come on you when wakened in the middle of the night by these human spirits. One way that you may be able to identify that one of these astral travelers has projected into your homes is by the foul smell that can attend their presence. Do not be surprised if you find things moved around in your homes. This can happen, but you should not allow it to continue. We have God's power to deal with it very simply through our prayers.

Each of these experiences is for our training. God is in the business of teaching His children His ways and the ways of the spirit realm. Trust in the Lord and allow Him to be your instructor. You do not have to figure out "why" this happened or worry about these types of encounters. If God wants you to do something more specific, He will tell you. Otherwise, just pray and be observant of what it is that God is teaching.

The way we learn, from childhood on, is by repetition. Today's lesson may only be an introduction, and each subsequent encounter a fuller revealing of what the Lord is teaching you. Be patient! Be a student of God!

81

---

^{vi} For an explanation of the doctrine of the Seven Spirits see *Manual of the Seven Spirits,* by Pastor Ron Crawford.

Discernment in the Heavens

Go Where Jesus Is

In my Father's house are many mansions: if it were not so, I would have told you. I go to prepare a place for you. ³And if I go and prepare a place for you, I will come again, and receive you unto myself; that where I am, there ye may be also.
—JOHN 14:2-3

Jesus said that He was going to go and prepare a place for us and that where He was we would be with Him. We should be very grateful that the apostle John realized how essential it was to abide in the Lord. He took great care to record the loving words of Jesus that were spoken during His last days on this earth.

Time and again, Jesus encouraged His disciples that they were to be one with Him as He was one with His Father. Jesus recognized that for His disciples to really have an intimate relationship with Him, they would have to be trained to abide with Him.

Through the years the Lord has been gracious to teach many of us how to abide with Him. As you set aside time each day to commune with the Lord, He will be faithful to draw you into His presence and teach you about His Kingdom.

We have personally experienced a marked increase in discernment through committing to a lifestyle of intercession. We have also witnessed many others within our congregation and many from other churches that have been blessed in this way.

One of the main purposes of this book is to encourage you to commit your life to prayer, and through that wonderful commitment, to see you step into discerning the deeper things of the Lord. Daily as you walk with Him, the Lord is preparing you to be able to discern. He wants you to witness the amazing things that are beginning to occur within His church, as well as the tremendous changes going on in the spiritual atmosphere of this world.

In a previous book, *Ministering from Our Heavenly Seats*, we attempted to describe some of the incredible things that are currently happening in the second heavens. Many of us will have to allow the Holy Spirit to stretch us out of our comfort zones to accept the fact that many unique and strange things exist in the heavenly realms.

In many ways, the Lord is activating our discernment so that we can have access to Him and these heavenly places. Our Heavenly Father is about to reveal to His church a network of communication centers and battle stations in the second heavens. Our Lord Jesus, the archangel Michael and his powerful corps of angels are preparing the saints to go to war. There is a major confrontation looming in the horizon between Satan, his seven princes and the other fallen angels against the Lord and His mighty army. This war will occur in the heavens, but in time will have major ramifications for the earth. Scripture says the fallen angels will be cast out of the heavens and onto the earth.

> *And there was war in heaven:* **Michael** *and his angels fought against the dragon; and the dragon fought and his angels,* *[8]And prevailed not; neither was their place found any more in heaven. [9]And the great dragon was cast out, that old serpent, called the Devil, and Satan, which deceiveth the whole world: he was cast out into the earth, and his angels were cast out with him.* —REVELATION 12:7-9

Currently, many saints have begun their special training for operating in these realms. There have been impressive weapons crafted for us that have extraordinary power against the forces of darkness. The Word of God is very clear that our weapons are not carnal and they are not of this world. The weapons that have been created for us are very high-tech, yet at the same time they are spiritual.

(For the weapons of our warfare are not carnal, but mighty through God to the pulling down of strong holds;)
—2 CORINTHIANS 10:4

You will be astounded when the Lord allows you to see how some of these saints are being outfitted. Some of the saints have been equipped with special helmets and eyewear not even Hollywood could script. Depending on your responsibilities in the heavenly places, the Lord gives you unique devices to use. Some of these devices are used to measure and make special calculations in places that the Lord is preparing for His saints. As you step by faith into functioning in these places, your knowledge and abilities are increased enormously. You may only have an average I.Q. here on this earth, but as you move into the realms that you were literally made for and will spend the rest of eternity in, you will discover that you can do anything that the Lord asks you to do.

I can do all things through Christ which strengtheneth me.
—PHILIPPIANS 4:13

The training we are receiving as saints is to equip us to work alongside the angels of the Lord. Satan and his angels have powerful weapons. Rest assured as saints, we will fall behind in no area of expertise. The Lord is preparing us to move as lightening as His angels do, and more importantly, as His sons do.

And the Lord shall be seen over them, and his arrow shall go forth as the lightning: and the Lord God shall blow the trumpet, and shall go with whirlwinds of the south.
—ZECHARIAH 9:14

As arrows are in the hand of a mighty man; so are children of the youth. ⁵Happy is the man that hath his quiver full of them: they shall not be ashamed, but they shall speak with the enemies in the gate.   —PSALM 127:4-5

As eyes are opened to the second heavens, it will become painfully obvious that the enemy has been showing those that follow him aspects of these realms for many years. More and more movies in Hollywood are depicting very accurately the things that go on in these realms. In addition, many of the beings that are put on screen very closely portray these fallen angels.

For those that press into the Lord with no hidden agendas, He will reveal to them His mysteries and teach them how to prepare for the days ahead.

The general churchgoer may have difficulty believing what has been related here and therefore, may not accept the things we have been sharing. Jesus said that many would be called to the marriage, but there would also be many that would not accept His invitation. In fact, there would be those who would make light of the whole proceeding.

> The kingdom of heaven is like unto a certain king, which made a marriage for his son, *³And sent forth his servants to call them that were bidden to the wedding: and **they would not come**. ⁴Again, he sent forth other servants, saying, Tell them which are bidden, Behold, I have prepared my dinner: my oxen and my fatlings are killed, and all things are ready: come unto the marriage. ⁵But they **made light of it**, and **went their ways**, one to his farm, another to his merchandise:*
> *—MATTHEW 22:2-5*

It says that there will be some that make light of those that go into the marriage supper. Will the general church make light of those who dare to make themselves ready to enter this wonderful place of supping with the Lord?

> Behold, I stand at the door, and knock: if any man hear my voice, and open the door, I will come in to him, and will **sup** with him, and he with me.
> *—REVELATION 3:20*

Unfortunately, a great majority of the church teaches and preaches on the perks of serving God. Bookstores are full of books, and the airwaves are full of voices clamoring for a chance to tell everyone about how they need to exercise their faith to be able to step into a more prosperous life. Jesus regularly talked about dying to self. Jesus did not want us worrying about tomorrow. He wanted His followers to be totally consumed with love for and absolute obedience to His Father.

The saints are those who have been called out from the general church and have shed their religious clothing. Daily they take up their crosses and follow hard after the Lord. They are determined to go deeper into the things of God. Saints are committed to His purposes and have said goodbye to the cares of this world. These heavenly-minded believers have become aliens in this world and feel more at home in the heavenlies.

The marriage supper of the Lamb is being made ready. The location of this supper will not be a surprise for those who are dear to the heart of the Lord. According to the Word, those who desire to be present at this marriage supper must be clothed in the right garments.

And when the king came in to see the guests, he saw there a man which had not on a wedding garment: [12]And he saith unto him, Friend, how camest thou in hither not having a wedding garment? And he was speechless.
—MATTHEW 22:11-12

The word "saints" means holy ones. The identifying color of the saint's garments is white. The white represents the saintly calling. It identifies those that are willing to give their lives for the Lord.

Thou hast a few names even in Sardis which have not defiled their garments; and they shall walk with me in white: for they are worthy. [5]He that overcometh, the same shall be clothed in white raiment; and I will not blot out his name out of the book of life, but I will confess his name before my Father, and before his angels.
—REVELATION 3:4-5

And one of the elders answered, saying unto me, What are these which are arrayed in white robes? and whence came they? [14]And I said unto him, Sir, thou knowest. And he said to me, These are they which came out of great tribulation, and have washed their robes, and made them white in the blood of the Lamb.
—REVELATION 7:13-14

And to her was granted that she should be arrayed in fine linen, clean and white: for the fine linen is the righteousness of saints.
—REVELATION 19:8

The saints will be very active in the last days and especially during the tribulation.

Until the Ancient of days came, and judgment was given to the saints of the most High; and the time came that the saints possessed the kingdom. —*DANIEL 7:22*

And he shall speak great words against the most High, and shall wear out the saints of the most High, and think to change times and laws: and they shall be given into his hand until a time and times and the dividing of time.
—*DANIEL 7:25*

And it was given unto him to make war with the saints, and to overcome them: and power was given him over all kindreds, and tongues, and nations.
—*REVELATION 13:7*

Here is the patience of the saints: here are they that keep the commandments of God, and the faith of Jesus.
—*REVELATION 14:12*

For they have shed the blood of saints and prophets, and thou hast given them blood to drink; for they are worthy.
—*REVELATION 16:6*

And I saw the woman drunken with the blood of the saints, and with the blood of the martyrs of Jesus: and when I saw her, I wondered with great admiration.
—*REVELATION 17:6*

And in her was found the blood of prophets, and of saints, and of all that were slain upon the earth.
—*REVELATION 18:24*

There are a lot of people who are counting on the rapture to get them off the earth before the fury of God is unleashed. However, when you read through the book of Revelation, you begin to realize the saints are still doing all kinds of things here on earth on behalf of the Father during the tribulation. Perhaps it is time for you to reconsider what we have always been taught about the rapture of the church.

The best thing for believers to do is what John the Beloved did. He found a place right next to the heart of the Lord. Each of us needs to find that abiding place and begin listening to what the Lord is really saying about the last days. The Lord is not giving different plans to different believers about what He is going to do in these last days. His church will operate at a level of unity that it has never before experienced. Crucial to all this is our ability to discern what He is telling us and showing us.

As we begin operating in the heavenly realms and functioning from the authority of our heavenly seats, we can only imagine the disdain that the saints will incur. The general church does not want to hear about dying to self, enduring tribulation and laying down our lives for our Lord. The most unusual and peculiar days for the church are upon us. As you step into operating in the spirit realm, there may be times when you may think you have lost your mind. However, just know that you are not alone. Remember, God's ways are foolish to man.

God is preparing us, step-by-step, to effectively battle in conjunction with His angels against the armies of darkness. Michael and his divisions are a very sober bunch. They are masterful at what they do, and they have certain expectations for those that minister alongside them. They expect us to be able to perform in the area God has placed us. The angels also understand the necessity of the prayer life of the saint. It is imperative that we have constant fellowship and commune with the Lord to be able to move into the places that we have been discussing.

Where is all this headed? The Lord is preparing His body to take their rightful positions in the heavens. Fighting along with Michael, they will evict Satan and his angels from these heavenly places. They will also ensure the enemy stays on the earth until the time for his judgment and casting into hell comes. The Lord is using the intercession of His humble servants to get ready for these end time events.

And there appeared another wonder in heaven; and behold a great red dragon, having seven heads and ten horns, and seven crowns upon his heads. ⁴And his tail drew the third part of the stars of heaven, and did cast them to the earth: . . .
—REVELATION 12:3-4

And the great dragon was cast out, that old serpent, called the Devil, and Satan, which deceiveth the whole world: he was cast out into the earth, and his angels were cast out with him.
—REVELATION 12:9

The Lord is gathering together a people that will be His ambassadors and spokesmen here upon the earth during these very trying days. The saints and sons of the Most High know their destiny. They are not afraid of imprisonment, torture or even death. They have tasted of eternity and know that their Lord will be with them. There is nothing to fear.

Stephen faced some dire circumstances when he was being accused, threatened and eventually stoned to death. However, even as he was being stoned, his attention was on the Lord.

> *But he, being full of the Holy Ghost, looked up stedfastly into heaven, and saw the glory of God, and Jesus standing on the right hand of God, [56]And said, Behold, I see the heavens opened, and the Son of man standing on the right hand of God.*
> —*ACTS 7:55-56*

So it must be with us. Our attention ever focused on the Lord.

Discerning the Purposes of Angels

God created the angels for many different purposes. One of their main functions is to partner with man to redeem this earth. The word "angel" means messenger, and although this is not their only function, throughout the Bible it was very common for the angels to communicate a special message from the Heavenly Father. On most of these occasions the Lord sent His angels to communicate a message or revelation from Him to those who had been chosen by the Lord to fulfill His purposes.

Think of Abraham's visit with the angels going to destroy Sodom (Genesis 18). It was an angel that led Moses and the Children of Israel through the wilderness (Exodus 23:20). Zacharias was visited in the temple with a word about the birth and upbringing of John the Baptist (Luke 1). In each of these examples, an angel came with a message about the fulfillment of God's purpose. And this is only a small portion of the many recorded in scripture.

Angelic messages can be very simple in nature. Sometimes angels simply tell us where we are supposed to pray in our sanctuary. On other occasions, directions are given to turn to a specific passage of scripture. Many times they come with fresh insights of passages that have previously been studied.

Considering the times in which we are living, it should not surprise anyone that there is an increase in the number of angelic visitations being reported. Angels visited Daniel several times with revelations of the last days. At one point, he was told to seal up the book until the time of the end.

> But thou, O Daniel, shut up the words, and <u>seal the book, even</u> <u>to the time of the end</u>: many shall run to and fro, and knowledge shall be increased. —DANIEL 12:4

We are living in those last days, and the Lord is opening up the book and revealing the mysteries that are within it. Our heavenly Father is sending His angels to make sure there will be complete understanding of these mysteries.

No doubt saints around the globe will be visited by angels in preparation for what God is going to do. It is the purpose of the Lord for His saints to take dominion of this earth. The angels are needed to aid us in our warfare against the fallen angels.

> And the kingdom and dominion, and the greatness of the kingdom under the whole heaven, shall be given to the people of the saints of the most High, whose kingdom is an everlasting kingdom, and all dominions shall serve and obey him. —DANIEL 7:27

> And there was war in heaven: Michael and his angels fought against the dragon; and the dragon fought and his angels, —REVELATION 12:7

Another example of the types of messages angels bring is simply those of directions. One day, my senior pastor and I were in downtown Dallas praying and preparing for an upcoming prophetic activation. We were trying to decide where the Lord wanted us to go and position ourselves. My pastor said, "Paul, do you know where we need to do this activation?" I did not know either. A few minutes later he said, "I know where we are supposed to go". I asked him how he knew. He said that there was an angel on a nearby hill, and he was pointing to the location.

Again the scriptures give us examples of this type of interaction. Remember the angel who told Philip to take the road to Gaza (Acts 8:26), and the angels at Jesus' tomb who tell the disciples to go into Galilee (Matthew 28:5-7).

Angelic Encounters

God is teaching the saints to know when the angels have come and how to communicate with them. This "knowing" will be accomplished by the gift of discerning of spirits and the communicating by the gift of divers tongues.

The angels themselves will carry out much of this training. In Hebrews, it talks about the angels coming and ministering for those who would be heirs of salvation. Ministering encompasses a great many things. It can mean to serve, to impart, to administer, to furnish or supply, to communicate, to prompt or to suggest. Many times angels come to share revelation and mysteries that will teach us more about God and His ways. Think of Daniel, Ezekiel and of John, all of whom received revelations from God brought to them by angels.

Angels come to our congregation on a regular basis. They have shared some of the most incredible revelations from the Word and have taken many of us in the spirit to visit places in the heavenlies that were totally outside the realm of our previous experiences. These are not extra-biblical revelations, but fresh understanding of scriptures that have been passed over because we did not comprehend them. First Peter calls these things "present truths". For more understanding of this topic, see *No New Thing* by Joy Harrison.

Angels come with both giftings and empowerment from the Lord. They also come to do battle with us in various spiritual arenas. Throughout the Bible we have examples of how angels came to deliver God's people. Today's church tends to limit this protection aspect of the angelic to the prevention of car accidents and near mishaps. Even though this is a function of angels, they spend much more time and energy moving on behalf of the saints to accomplish the Lord's purposes in this hour.

Recently, a team from our church was sent out to minister in France. We were driving together in a large rented van to the church we were scheduled to minister at that morning just outside of Paris. All of a sudden, an angel appeared at the side window of the van and told us to be very careful because it was dangerous ahead. A few moments later, we started noticing terrible wrecks all over the freeway. We could not see any ice, but apparently the road had patches of "black ice" all over it. We lost count of all the wrecks we saw. We finally came to a place on the road, which had a barricade and detour sign. The authorities finally closed the highway because of the potential hazards. We thanked the Lord for protecting us from having an untimely accident.

Angelic Personalities

An interesting aspect that these angelic encounters have revealed is that angels have emotions and personalities. From our narrow perspective as believers, we assume angels are just alike in their constitution, basically clones. That is certainly a mistake.

Angels can be joyful, sometimes even hilarious. Certain angels have an amazing anointing of joy, and when they enter your prayer times or services the people could very easily break out into a holy laughter. The angels rejoiced at the birth of Jesus, and they also rejoice when sinners get saved.

Other angels can ignite people to begin worshipping and praising God. Their anointing is often characterized by jubilant shouts and accompanied by exuberant dance and worship. We call these the Judah angels. When they come there is usually an eruption of worship.

There are angels who exude the very passionate love of the Lord. When they come, you sense God's very presence and often hear the reassuring message that the Lord loves you. There are even angels that the Lord sends to befriend and walk with you for a season.

On the other hand, when warring angels come, the tone of the service will grow very serious. Your tongues often become very harsh and deliberate, while at the same time the spiritual atmosphere becomes very intense. These warring angels are led by Michael, the Captain of the Lord's hosts, so we refer to them as the Michael Corp. It is amazing, depending on which corps of angels the Lord sends, how the spiritual climate changes during a time of intercession.

We have already spoken of the messenger function of angels. Gabriel leads the angelic corps especially tasked with communicating the ways of God. The best descriptions of Gabriel come from the booklet *Gabriel* by Pastor Ron Crawford.

In seeking to describe Gabriel to you, quoting from his work is best. "The ministry of Gabriel has always been one of exact adherence to the ways of God. In fact, he is the messenger of the ways of the Heavenly Father. Everything about him indicates that this is the driving focus of his existence. While other angels were created to focus on various capacities of service to God, the ministry of Gabriel and his corps literally involves communicating what God is doing, as well as what He is about to do." (*Gabriel*, p. 1)

It seems like there are greater influxes of the angelic during corporate intercessory times. It is amazing how a group of people can be stirred identically depending on which angels have been sent.

You will learn that the angels flow with the established authority in the house. In the beginning the angels will flow through the senior pastor or leader. This is not to say that the angels will not visit the various members in the church. However, when the angels have been sent on assignment into a church, they will flow through the authority structure that has been established.

You will read books or hear about different individuals who have had visitations from angels. If anyone claims to direct angels in a ministry situation and they are not the senior leader in the church or given direct authority to do so by the senior leader, a red flag should go up. If they say that angels are carrying out major operations from their home, be wary. God works through His church, not through lone rangers operating outside of the body of Christ.

My prayer is that all of us would be more sensitive to the presence of the Lord's angels. They come to assist the saints in what God has called them to do. We must flow in the gift of discernment so that we can partner with them.

We must purpose to walk with the Lord and operate in His Kingdom. It is not enough to just see angels or sense their presence. We must learn how to communicate and work with them. This takes discernment and it also takes great faith. The Lord has been very gracious to send some of His very powerful angels to our church.

One of the things the Lord has taught us over the last couple of years is that when He tells you to do something you need to do it. Do it in His timing and exactly the way He directs it to be done.

Angels of the Lord honor authority; it is part of their makeup. When they visit a church, they flow through the existing authority. That is why it is so important that a church have a proper flow of authority in its leadership. The angels flow through the senior pastor or leader down to the rest of the congregation.

The Lord's angels will not move with anyone who is in rebellion. It will not happen. If a person in rebellion is interacting with angels, you can be assured they are dealing with fallen angels.

There are many types of heavenly angels, and only a few of them are mentioned here. This is not about knowing all the different kinds of angels. It is about understanding how God's Kingdom works. Every one of these angels has a very specific role and function to perform in God's Kingdom. All are completely focused and absorbed in accomplishing their tasks toward establishing the purposes of God. If angels could be summarized in one statement, it would be "Focused on God and His purpose." Nothing distracts them from that all-consuming motivation.

As you seek to discern, we echo the Apostle Paul's prayer for you.

> *Wherefore I also, after I heard of your faith in the Lord Jesus, and love unto all the saints, [16]Cease not to give thanks for you, making mention of you in my prayers; [17]That the God of our Lord Jesus Christ, the Father of glory, may give unto you the spirit of wisdom and revelation in the knowledge of him: [18]The eyes of your understanding being enlightened; that ye may know what is the hope of his calling, and what the riches of the glory of his inheritance in the saints, [19]And what is the exceeding greatness of his power to us-ward who believe, according to the working of his mighty power, [20]Which he wrought in Christ, when he raised him from the dead, and set him at his own right hand in the heavenly places, [21]Far above all principality, and power, and might, and dominion, and every name that is named, not only in this world, but also in that which is to come: [22]And hath put all things under his feet, and gave him to be the head over all things to the church, [23]Which is his body, the fulness of him that filleth all in all.*
> *—EPHESIANS 1:15-23*

Encounters with Heavenly Believers

There are many different beings in the heavenlies; thus far we have dealt with only two groups. We have talked of God's angels and of the fallen angels.

The Bible also refers to the Four Living Creatures or the Four Beasts, and the elders. Other than believing they exist and do interact with us, we are not going to review these groups. However, there is one group which is often found in the heavens and which many believers question. This group consists of those individuals who have passed from this earth and are now with the Lord; individuals beginning with Adam and including all those in between right up to the saint of God who passed on to eternity today.

This area causes much discussion among believers and is addressed in detail in a later chapter.

7

Discerning Fallen Angels

Angels of Light

As wonderful as it is to interact with God's angels, there are also fallen angels. Often believers will avoid the chance of deception by avoiding angelic encounters all together. On the other extreme, are those who accept every angelic encounter as godly. They are gullible, believing every spirit that shows up. Both of these approaches are foolishness. The first is like the man who will not use a motor vehicle, because someday he might be in an accident. The second approach is like the man who gives his ten year old, untrained son the keys to his high-performance sports car. Both result in God's will being delayed or derailed for that individual's life.

Angels are God-given co-laborers in His Kingdom. Without them, God's purposes will not be accomplished. So instead of avoiding or embracing all angelic encounters, it is time to search the scriptures and determine what the Lord says about this crucial topic. We must know what God says about angels, or we will be deceived. So please set aside all your preconceived notions and open your hearts, like the Bereans, to find out the truth. The Word of God must be our final authority in the subject at hand and it is imperative that we be not deceived.

And no marvel; for Satan himself is transformed into an angel of light. [15]*Therefore it is no great thing if his ministers also be transformed as the ministers of righteousness; whose end shall be according to their works.*

—2 CORINTHIANS 11:14-15

It is significant for our discussion that we clarify what we mean when we refer to demons and dark angels. Demons are fallen angels who have been restricted to this earth. In the authority structure of the demonic realm they populate the lowest ranks in the kingdom of darkness. Basically they inhabit people, places and objects. They are ruled by principalities and powers and ultimately do whatever they are told. They represent the soldiers in the army of evil. They practice terrorizing and tempting individuals. In addition, demons are responsible for a great portion of the sickness and disease on the earth.

Dark angels are also fallen angels, but have greater authority and tend to reside in the second heavens. The Apostle Paul refers to these fallen angels as principalities, powers, rulers of darkness, and spiritual wickedness in high places.

For we wrestle not against flesh and blood, but against **principalities**, *against* **powers**, *against the* **rulers of the darkness** *of this world, against* **spiritual wickedness** *in high places.* *—EPHESIANS 6:12*

And having spoiled **principalities** *and* **powers**, *he made a shew of them openly, triumphing over them in it.*

—COLOSSIANS 2:15

These dark angels govern the various regions of the earth. Through their coordinated efforts, they resist God's intended purpose for the territories over which they exercise control. Most of them rule in places where God wants to establish His saints in dominion.

Even though this is not a book on deliverance, it is important to know that there is an entirely different way to deal with demons than with dark angels. Demons can and should be "cast out" and individuals delivered in the timing and under the direction of the Lord. Dark angels do not "inhabit" people, places and objects, but rather rule over territories. It takes battle to dislodge them and dismantle their evil strongholds.

One thing the Lord has taught us is not to react to the demonic so quickly. In the past, we thought if we discerned something evil we needed to do something about it right away. We have since learned that everything must be done in the Lord's perfect timing, and that would definitely include deliverance and even more imperatively, spiritual warfare.

Many times our immediate reaction to help someone who is demonized comes from an overactive mercy gifting. However, if we do not consult the Lord first, then we may find ourselves operating in soulish mercy. We tend to forget Jesus' exhortation that if somebody does not clean the house after deliverance, then seven demons come back to attack the person. At times we generate a far worse scenario for people by delivering them outside of the timing of God even though our intentions are genuinely for their good.

Demons act on the orders of their superiors, always attempting to undermine the purposes of God in people and places. For individuals, demons try to keep them from fulfilling God's destiny in their lives. The enemy can see the many gifts and callings on people, and he is determined to twist them for his own purposes. The twisting of godly purpose results in iniquities in our lives. One of the aspects of the work that Jesus did on the cross was being "bruised for our iniquities." Through His life, death and resurrection, He gave us power to be set free from the twisting the enemy had made in God's purposes for our lives.

As we move in greater discernment, the Lord wants us to be able to identify gifts and callings in each other's lives and to encourage those giftings. We need to identify these giftings and then train the individuals to use their giftings in God's Kingdom. For many people, all they have heard throughout their lives is negative things about themselves. That is not God's way, especially for our young people. We need to know what they were created for and declare God's purposes over them daily. We have allowed the enemy to kill, steal and destroy many of the young people in the church because we failed to identify and train them in their spiritual giftings.

As we said, demons are responsible for much of the illness and disease on the earth. However, not every sickness or disease is demonic. Many are the result of self-indulgent living. The important thing for us to remember is that whatever sickness the enemy brings against us, its ultimate target is to hinder us from doing what God has called us to do.

Besides physical attacks, demons are very busy causing mental disabilities, too. Many mental institutions are filled with people who simply need to be delivered. In these days, we must have our minds protected from the onslaught of the enemy. The Word is filled with verses about having the mind of Christ and protecting our minds.

And be **renewed** *in the spirit of your* **mind;**
—EPHESIANS 4:23

Let this **mind** *be in you, which was also in Christ Jesus:*
—PHILIPPIANS 2:5

For God hath not given us the spirit of fear; but of power, and of love, and of a **sound mind.**   *—2 TIMOTHY 1:7*

A keen sense of discernment is very crucial in the area of healing and deliverance. So often we are quick to lay hands on someone to pray for their healing. Often this is done without any inquiry of the Lord. Unfortunately, many of us would probably have been praying for Job and trying to break off all the things that were coming against him. If we had done so, we would have been going against the purpose of God for his life. We must be able to ascertain what the Spirit wants done in every situation. **Anyone can pray for someone's healing, but only those who are truly listening to the Father will not pray for deliverance until God says to pray.** It takes great courage to wait for instructions from heaven, especially when it seems that everybody is saying you should have mercy and pray for this poor person. We must obey the Lord in every aspect of our life. He is looking for servants who so trust Him that they will only do what He wants done.

In these last days, we must have the mind of Christ. The enemy will do everything he can to confuse and discourage us in our callings. We have witnessed numerous people who were chosen of the Lord endure the harassment of the enemy. They were attacked relentlessly in their minds, and without the mind of Christ, they began believing the lies they were being told.

Strife and Division

For where envying and strife is, there is confusion and every evil work.   *—JAMES 3:16*

There are countless ways the enemy uses to cause strife and division. The enemy is an expert at causing miscommunications among the brethren. Many times we have said one thing to someone, and the person left understanding a completely different message. We must realize that the enemy seeks to destroy relationships through this means.

A person can be gifted and called to accomplish the Lord's purposes in a particular church. It is very powerful, when a person is aligned with the part of the body of Christ that God intended. Whenever the enemy recognizes God's purposes in the process of fulfillment, he immediately begins devising ways to cause division. It can be a very simple thing. It can come by way of a parent taking offense at how their children were treated. It can come by way of how your friend in the church was somehow mistreated by a leader. It is amazing how quickly people take up the offenses of others. This is extremely dangerous. It tends to be those with mercy giftings that fall into this area of deception most often.

The enemy constantly seeds negative thoughts into our minds. If we do not do as the Apostle Paul says and cast these thoughts down, they could be our undoing. We have seen the most stable and mature saints bite into a lie of the enemy and be completely removed from the pathway to which God had called them. If we do not learn to distinguish the voice of the enemy, we will forever be susceptible to his ploys.

Paul also admonishes us, *"to put on the whole armor of God."* The purpose for this is to be able to *"stand against the wiles of the enemy."* In the Greek, the word "wiles" means "trickery or to lie in wait". The enemy very patiently waits to seduce us. He crafts very well thought out plans designed to destroy us or at the very least, knock us off course in our purpose in God. We must ask the Lord to give us the discernment necessary to identify these "wiles" of the enemy.

Standing against the devil means taking a proactive stance toward stopping what is coming against us. Knowing that the enemy is the father of all lies, you must stay alert. He will do his very best to attempt to turn you against your leaders and drive you away from the church where God has planted you. The goal of the enemy is to plant seeds of distrust in our minds with the intent of undermining our relationships with our leaders. Ultimately, the enemy would desire for you to act presumptuously and leave before you seek counsel from those who are in authority. We have to be determined to not allow the enemy to hinder what God has purposed for our lives. The enemy would much rather you blame leadership and leave the church instead of submitting as unto the Lord and waiting on the Lord to resolve whatever situation has troubled you.

If the enemy comes and tells you that leadership is holding you back, just remember how slow God moves when He is preparing His servants. Jesus spent the first thirty years of His life preparing, before His Father released Him into ministry. It has been estimated that the Apostle Paul was in the wilderness for twelve to fourteen years before he was launched into full-time ministry. Joseph waited in a prison for twenty years, David in a cave, Moses in a wilderness. As we stated earlier, patience is the first sign of the apostolic. When you hear a voice suggesting that you are not moving quickly enough, there is a high probability it is not the voice of the Lord. When He is ready for us to move, heaven and earth will move around us. There is no holding back His purpose being accomplished through us. Miracles catch us, Pharaohs call, and bushes burn. The Lord is all about developing relationships and teaching us to hear and know His voice.

Lucifer's Downfall: To Be Like God

I will ascend above the heights of the clouds; I will be like the most High. —ISAIAH 14:14

Lucifer wanted to be worshipped. Those that followed him out of heaven want to be worshipped as well. We have found that when a person is causing some disturbance in a service, the person is most likely being influenced by a demon. There is a story of a demon-possessed woman in Acts that followed the Apostle Paul around for several days. Paul ignored it for a while, but then he finally dealt with her.

And it came to pass, as we went to prayer, a certain damsel possessed with a spirit of divination met us, which brought her masters much gain by soothsaying: [17]The same followed Paul and us, and cried, saying, These men are the servants of the most high God, which shew unto us the way of salvation. [18]And this did she many days. But Paul, being grieved, turned and said to the spirit, I command thee in the name of Jesus Christ to come out of her. And he came out the same hour.
—ACTS 16:16-18

Often when people yell out during a service, it is critical that we are able to discern whether the person is demonic or simply has an emotional issue. Many times we have seen people start ministering deliverance to an individual when it was not necessary. When we make those types of mistakes, it usually causes confusion or fear to come upon the people.

Here again, the key is learning to set aside the outward physical manifestation and sensing whether something demonic is going on in the spirit. Too often the enemy succeeds in causing disruptions in our services, because we take the bait he has offered. If the pastor or leader is not going to minister to the individual at that time, then an usher might need to remove the person causing the disturbance.

Once the person is removed, then those that are ministering to them need to be able to discern the situation and determine how the person and the situation should be handled. Every church has their own way of dealing with disturbances, so we will not interfere with whatever method you have established. The important thing is to not let the demon gain a lot of attention through the disturbance.

On one occasion we were ministering in a church, and a person began manifesting in a most unusual way. The person began slithering on the floor like a snake. However, it was the reaction of some of the pastoral staff and ministry team that amazed us. There must have been six people chasing this slithering demoniac throughout the altar area. The ministry team was shouting and screaming at the demon and was causing quite a commotion themselves.

Jesus dealt very effectively with demoniacs. There was never a case where Jesus lost control of the situation. He spoke and moved with great authority when He was dealing with those who were in bondage to the enemy.

Authority within the Realm of Satan

The demonic hosts are under authority, not because they choose to be, but because God created them this way. The kingdom of darkness is not a free-for-all, where the demons can do whatever they want. They are under very strict control by their leaders.

But he, knowing their thoughts, said unto them, Every kingdom divided against itself is brought to desolation; and a house divided against a house falleth. [18]*If Satan also be divided against himself, how shall his kingdom stand? because ye say that I cast out devils through Beelzebub.*

—*LUKE 11:17-18*

When Jesus was responding to the skeptics, He made it very clear that the kingdom of darkness works in a unified fashion. The only way that you keep unity is to have an established authority structure and make certain everyone stays in rank. If the enemy's kingdom knows the importance of staying under authority, how much more should we as the church grasp this critical understanding?

When an individual or church determines to go hard after God, you can count on the enemy redeploying his troops to attempt to stop this forward progression. Sometimes we may think we have missed God, because we are running against so much interference in doing what the Lord has requested of us. Many times as leaders, we may be second-guessed for the course of action we have taken. Most believers do not want to have to engage the enemy in warfare. However, if you are planning to take dominion of the land with the Lord, there are going to be great battles to be fought.

Judging Angels

As we said in the beginning of this chapter, we must not believe every spirit. We are to judge spiritual encounters of all kinds.

Beloved, believe not every spirit, but try the spirits whether they are of God: because many false prophets are gone out into the world. —*1 JOHN 4:1*

Know ye not that we shall judge angels? how much more things that pertain to this life?

—*1 CORINTHIANS 6:3*

Several very non-scriptural deceptions have crept into the church in the last decade; all of which if examined in light of the Word of God would be revealed for the lies they are. Unfortunately, the thrill of interacting with angels has led many to lay aside the Word of God and rely totally on their experiences. We are going to examine some of these deceptions in the rest of this chapter.

Over the last several years there has been an increase in the reports of female angels making appearances in church services and conferences. Even though the reports of female angels were initially troubling, it was not our responsibility to teach on the subject, one way or the other. It was not until recently that the Lord initiated a study of the scriptures to find out for certain about the existence of female angels.

The Lord directed a study from Genesis through Revelation, examining every passage that referred to angels or angelic encounters. It was astounding to see the absolute certainty of God's Word on this topic. At the same time, we still did not wish to come across as having a critical heart toward other ministries. A critical spirit cannot only be divisive, but it can potentially destroy lives. However, the time came when the Lord commanded that the results of this study be shared.

Therefore, it is with great humility that this message is brought to you. The Father gave the following verses as a mandate for delivering this word to His body.

Again the word of the Lord came unto me, saying, ²Son of man, speak to the children of thy people, and say unto them, When I bring the sword upon a land, if the people of the land take a man of their coasts, and set him for their watchman: 3If when he seeth the sword come upon the land, he blow the trumpet, and warn the people; ⁴Then whosoever heareth the sound of the trumpet, and taketh not warning; if the sword come, and take him away, his blood shall be upon his own head. ⁵He heard the sound of the trumpet, and took not warning; his blood shall be upon him. But he that taketh warning shall deliver his soul. 6But if the watchman see the sword come, and blow not the trumpet, and the people be not warned; if the sword come, and take any person from among them, he is taken away in his iniquity; but his blood will I require at the watchman's hand. ⁷So thou, O son of man, I have set thee a watchman unto the house of Israel; therefore thou shalt hear the word at my mouth, and warn them from me. ⁸When I say unto the wicked, O wicked man, thou shalt surely die; if thou dost not speak to warn the wicked from his way, that wicked man shall die in his iniquity; but his blood will I require at thine hand. ⁹Nevertheless, if thou warn the wicked of his way to turn from it; if he do not turn from his way, he shall die in his iniquity; but thou hast delivered thy soul.　　　　　　　　　　　　*—EZEKIEL 33:1-9*

This is not about individual ministries, therefore the names of authors and ministries have purposely been left out. As an additional precaution to protect the anonymity of any individuals involved, quotations have been paraphrased, thus precluding the need for a bibliography. The sole purpose of this chapter is to warn the saints about the heretical teachings and revelations about angels that have crept into the church through books and conferences. It is a wise man who hears a warning of deception and seeks to know God's truth no matter who may be involved.

In addition to teachings about female angels, there are several other angelic teachings that directly contradict the Word of God. Each is addressed in this chapter. They include teachings about gender-based assignments, ages, names, wounded angels, child angels and the Seven Spirits of God as angels.

female Angels?

The most notable female angel being propagated across the United States today is known as Emma, the "angel of the prophetic." Touted as being the angel who birthed and ignited the prophetic movement in Kansas City in the 1980s, it is reported that she watched over and nurtured this movement as it developed.

Emma has been portrayed as very young and beautiful, appearing to be in her early twenties, and yet having an aura of great age and great wisdom. This angel is said to emit a brilliant light and colors and to carry bags containing gold dust which she sprinkles on people. Emma is purported to bring wealth and open up prophetic wells in the places to which she is invited. Wonderful manifestations have accompanied many of her appearances.

As an aside, we have been questioned whether or not we believe that gold dust is from the Lord. Scripture speaks clearly of such things and we do believe that God can and does demonstrate His glory through the manifestation of gold dust. To produce gold dust is certainly miraculous, but remember no manifestation or miracle is proof of divine favor or authorship.

While traveling recently in India, a young woman told us of her pilgrimage to visit a famous Hindu guru. One of the proofs this guru gives that he is a reincarnation of a Hindu god is to produce gold dust. Clearly, this is not a sign that this person is part of the Kingdom of Heaven. So in a situation where the one performing the spiritual manifestation does not align with God's Word, the manifestation is a false sign.

The question is, does Emma align with God's Word or not? If she is, as we believe, actually a fallen angel masquerading as an angel of light, then the gold dust should be considered a false sign and wonder.

As with any sign and wonder, we should always be careful not to pursue the sign. There are many people who go from conference to conference looking for gold dust, oil dripping from ministers' hands or even angel feathers. This is extremely dangerous and immature. Jesus criticized those that sought signs.

Then certain of the scribes and of the Pharisees answered, saying, Master, we would see a sign from thee. [39]But he answered and said unto them, An evil and adulterous generation seeketh after a sign; and there shall no sign be given to it, but the sign of the prophet Jonas:
—MATTHEW 12:38-39

Numerous ministries are welcoming Emma into their conferences. If she is of God, that would be wonderful. However, the scriptures will be the final judge of this question. Emma is not the only female angel making special appearances. One author has written several booklets chronicling his encounters with angels. He talks about several guardian angels that are female. One day the author asked one of the angels who regularly communicated with him whether he was male or female. The angel responded that he was both male and female. That statement was even more troubling.

These ministries and their welcoming of Emma and other female angels only serves to illustrate that in the last days men will follow seducing spirits and believe a lie. Please, do not believe us. Instead, examine the Word of God carefully with us in these next pages to see whether or not female angels or even bi-sexual angels can truly be of God. No logic, no feelings, no experiences are valid foundations for belief, only the Word of God.

The most predominant passage that is used for the existence of female angels is Zechariah 5:5-11. In the booklet, *Angels of Deception*, Pastor Ron Crawford does a masterful job of giving scriptural proof that this passage does not refer to godly angels but instead refers to demons.

Crawford says, "If this is the passage that is used to authorize feminine angelic messengers, we had better look at this again. These creatures are not doing a godly thing. They are transporting a demonic entity to a place that is not good." Zechariah says the purpose for the journey is to build the demon a house. God does not send His angels to build a house for demons.

We have discovered very few Christian books that denounce the existence of female angels. Most authors use the Zechariah 5 passage to justify their belief in female angels. In one book it even stated that male angels appear to men and female angels appear to women.

So let us look to the Word of God for the answer. The word angel or *"malak"* is first used in the Bible in the book of Genesis. In this particular passage, there is a very clear understanding of the gender of the angel who is sent to Hagar. In this passage it is very clear that a male angel visited a woman.

*And the **angel of the Lord** found her by a fountain of water in the wilderness, by the fountain in the way to Shur. [8]And **he** said, Hagar, Sarai's maid, whence camest thou? and whither wilt thou go? And she said, I flee from the face of my mistress Sarai.* —GENESIS 16:7-8

Next, the Lord sends two male angels to warn Lot and his family of the impending judgment.

*And there came **two angels** to Sodom at even; and Lot sat in the gate of Sodom: and Lot seeing them rose up to meet them; and he bowed himself with his face toward the ground;... [10]But the **men** put forth their hand, and pulled Lot into the house to them, and shut to the door. [11]And they smote the men that were at the door of the house with blindness, both small and great: so that they wearied themselves to find the door.* —GENESIS 19:1,10-11

Now let us move on to Jacob's famous fight with an angel. Although at first glance this Genesis passage appears ambiguous about whether Jacob wrestled with a man or an angel, the parallel scripture in Hosea makes the meaning unmistakable it was a male angel.

*And Jacob went on his way, and the **angels of God** met him.* —GENESIS 32:1

*And Jacob was left alone; and there wrestled a **man** with him until the breaking of the day.* —GENESIS 32:24

*The Lord hath also a controversy with Judah, and will punish Jacob according to his ways; according to his doings will he recompense him. ³He took his brother by the heel in the womb, and by his strength he had power with God: ⁴Yea, he had power over the **angel**, and prevailed: he wept, and made supplication unto him: he found **him** in Bethel, and there **he** spake with us;* —HOSEA 12:2-4

The next several passages continue to depict angels as being male whether they appeared to men like Balaam and Gideon or to a woman like Samson's mother.

Balaam encounters an angel.

*And God's anger was kindled because he went: and the **angel of the Lord** stood in the way for an adversary against him. Now he was riding upon his ass, and his two servants were with him. ²³And the ass saw the **angel** of the Lord standing in the way, and **his** sword drawn in **his** hand: and the ass turned aside out of the way, and went into the field: and Balaam smote the ass, to turn her into the way.* —NUMBERS 22:22-23

An angel appears to Gideon.

*And there came an **angel of the Lord**, and sat under an oak which was in Ophrah, that pertained unto Joash the Abi-ezrite: and his son Gideon threshed wheat by the winepress, to hide it from the Midianites. ¹²And the **angel of the Lord** appeared unto him, and said unto him, The Lord is with thee, thou mighty man of valour. ¹³And Gideon said unto **him**, Oh my Lord, if the Lord be with us, why then is all this befallen us? and where be all his miracles which our fathers told us of, saying, Did not the Lord bring us up from Egypt? but now the Lord hath forsaken us, and delivered us into the hands of the Midianites.* —JUDGES 6:11-13

An angel appears to Samson's mother.

*And the **angel of the Lord** appeared unto the woman, and said unto her, Behold now, thou art barren, and bearest not: but thou shalt conceive, and bear a son. ⁴Now therefore beware, I pray thee, and drink not wine nor strong drink, and eat not any unclean thing: ⁵For, lo, thou shalt conceive, and bear a son; and no razor shall come on his head: for the child shall be a Nazarite unto God from the womb: and he shall begin to deliver Israel out of the hand of the Philistines. ⁶Then the woman came and told her husband, saying, **A man of God** came unto me, and **his** countenance was like the countenance of an angel of God, very terrible: but I asked **him** not whence **he** was, neither told **he** me **his** name:*
—JUDGES 13:3-6

An angel smites the people.

*And when the **angel** stretched out **his** hand upon Jerusalem to destroy it, the Lord repented him of the evil, and said to the angel that destroyed the people, It is enough: stay now thine hand. And the **angel of the Lord** was by the threshingplace of Araunah the Jebusite.*   —2 SAMUEL 24:16

Although the verses in Zechariah are regularly misused for the rationalization of female angels, there are many other verses in the Book of Zechariah that make it very obvious that angels are indeed male. In addition to the verses quoted below, all other angelic references in Zechariah show angels in the male gender. They include Zechariah 2:3; 4:1, 6; 5:5, 6; 6:4-5, 8.

*And I said unto the **angel** that talked with me, What be these? And **he** answered me, These are the horns which have scattered Judah, Israel, and Jerusalem.*
—ZECHARIAH 1:19

*Then said I, What come these to do? And **he** spake, saying, These are the horns which have scattered Judah, so that no man did lift up his head: but these are come to fray them, to cast out the horns of the Gentiles, which lifted up their horn over the land of Judah to scatter it.*
—ZECHARIAH 1:21

Someone might conjecture that since we have entered the dispensation of the new covenant that if female angels existed, God may have decided to start revealing them. Let us see what the New Testament scripture reveals.

Gabriel appears to Zacharias and Mary.

*And there appeared unto him an **angel of the Lord** standing on the right side of the altar of incense. [12]And when Zacharias saw **him**, he was troubled, and fear fell upon him. . . . [18]And Zacharias said unto the **angel**, Whereby shall I know this? for I am an old man, and my wife well stricken in years. [19]And the angel answering said unto him, I am **Gabriel**, that stand in the presence of God; and am sent to speak unto thee, and to shew thee these glad tidings.* —LUKE 1:11-12, 18-19

Notice that in each of the following examples, there is a reference to the masculine gender of the angel.

An angel rolls back the stone.

*And, behold, there was a great earthquake: for the **angel of the Lord** descended from heaven, and came and rolled back the stone from the door, and sat upon it. [3]**His** countenance was like lightning, and **his** raiment white as snow:* —MATTHEW 28:2-3

An angel visits Cornelius.

*He saw in a vision evidently about the ninth hour of the day an **angel of God** coming in to him, and saying unto him, Cornelius. [4]And when he looked on **him**, he was afraid, and said, What is it, Lord? And **he** said unto him, Thy prayers and thine alms are come up for a memorial before God.* —ACTS 10:3-4

*And Cornelius said, Four days ago I was fasting until this hour; and at the ninth hour I prayed in my house, and, behold, a **man** stood before me in bright clothing,* —ACTS 10:30

An angel frees Peter from prison.

*And, behold, the **angel of the Lord** came upon him, and a light shined in the prison: and **he** smote Peter on the side, and raised him up, saying, Arise up quickly. And his chains fell off from his hands. [8]And the **angel** said unto him, Gird thyself, and bind on thy sandals. And so he did. And **he** saith unto him, Cast thy garment about thee, and follow me. [9]And he went out, and followed **him**; and wist not that it was true which was done by **the angel**; but thought he saw a vision.*
—*ACTS 12:7- 9*

The Book of Revelation is full of angelic references. In fact, it contains the most prolific accounts of angels in the entire Bible. If there is any book in the Bible that should provide us with the characteristics of the angelic, the Book of Revelation is it.

*And after these things I saw four **angels** standing on the four corners of the earth, holding the four winds of the earth, that the wind should not blow on the earth, nor on the sea, nor on any tree. [2]And I saw another **angel** ascending from the east, having the seal of the living God: and **he** cried with a loud voice to the four angels, to whom it was given to hurt the earth and the sea,*
—*REVELATION 7:1-2*

*And I saw the seven **angels** which stood before God; and to them were given seven trumpets. [3]And another **angel** came and stood at the altar, having a golden censer; and there was given unto **him** much incense, that **he** should offer it with the prayers of all saints upon the golden altar which was before the throne.*
—*REVELATION 8:2-3*

*And the fifth **angel** sounded, and I saw a star fall from heaven unto the earth: and to **him** was given the key of the bottomless pit. [2]And **he** opened the bottomless pit; and there arose a smoke out of the pit, as the smoke of a great furnace; and the sun and the air were darkened by reason of the smoke of the pit.*
—*REVELATION 9:1-2*

*And I saw another mighty **angel** come down from heaven, clothed with a cloud: and a rainbow was upon **his** head, and **his** face was as it were the sun, and **his** feet as pillars of fire:*
                                        —REVELATION 10:1

*And I went unto the **angel**, and said unto **him**, Give me the little book. And **he** said unto me, Take it, and eat it up; and it shall make thy belly bitter, but it shall be in thy mouth sweet as honey.*   *—REVELATION 10:9*

*And another **angel** came out of the temple which is in heaven, **he** also having a sharp sickle.*
                                        —REVELATION 14:17

Revelation 16 describes the sequence of seven angels that pour out the vials of God's wrath. If there were ever an opportunity for God to do something without partiality to gender, it would be here.

*And I heard a great voice out of the temple saying to the seven **angels**, Go your ways, and pour out the vials of the wrath of God upon the earth. ²And the **first** went, and poured out **his** vial upon the earth; and there fell a noisome and grievous sore upon the men which had the mark of the beast, and upon them which worshipped his image. ³And the **second angel** poured out **his** vial upon the sea; and it became as the blood of a dead man: and every living soul died in the sea. ⁴And the **third angel** poured out **his** vial upon the rivers and fountains of waters; and they became blood.*
                                        —REVELATION 16:1-4

*And the **fourth angel** poured out **his** vial upon the sun; and power was given unto **him** to scorch men with fire.*
                                        —REVELATION 16:8

*And the **fifth angel** poured out **his** vial upon the seat of the beast; and his kingdom was full of darkness; and they gnawed their tongues for pain,*   *—REVELATION 16:10*

*And the **sixth angel** poured out **his** vial upon the great river Euphrates; and the water thereof was dried up, that the way of the kings of the east might be prepared.*
—REVELATION 16:12

*And the **seventh angel** poured out **his** vial into the air; and there came a great voice out of the temple of heaven, from the throne, saying, It is done. —REVELATION 16:17*

We close out Revelation with three examples of angels, all of which are described in the male gender.

*And after these things I saw another **angel** come down from heaven, having great power; and the earth was lightened with **his** glory. —REVELATION 18:1*

*And I saw an **angel** standing in the sun; and **he** cried with a loud voice, saying to all the fowls that fly in the midst of heaven, Come and gather yourselves together unto the supper of the great God; —REVELATION 19:17*

*And I saw an **angel** come down from heaven, having the key of the bottomless pit and a great chain in **his** hand. [2]And **he** laid hold on the dragon, that old serpent, which is the Devil, and Satan, and bound him a thousand years,*
—REVELATION 20:1-2

The only two angels of the Lord that God mentions by name are Michael and Gabriel. Notice that both of these high-ranking angels are male.

*Yet **Michael the archangel**, when contending with the devil **he** disputed about the body of Moses, durst not bring against him a railing accusation, but said, The Lord rebuke thee.*
—JUDE 1:9

*Yea, whiles I was speaking in prayer, even **the man Gabriel**, whom I had seen in the vision at the beginning, being caused to fly swiftly, touched me about the time of the evening oblation. —DANIEL 9:21*

Additionally, scripture teaches about two other classifications of angels, cherubim and seraphim. The Holy Spirit, once again made certain we knew the gender of these types of angels.

*And one **cherub** stretched forth **his** hand from between the cherubims unto the fire that was between the cherubims, and took thereof, and put it into the hands of him that was clothed with linen: who took it, and went out. [8]And there appeared in the **cherubims** the form of a **man's** hand under their wings.*
—*EZEKIEL 10:7-8*

*Above it stood the **seraphims**: each one had six wings; with twain **he** covered **his** face, and with twain **he** covered **his** feet, and with twain **he** did fly.* —*ISAIAH 6:2*

Even all of the dark angels mentioned in scripture are male. It should be noted as you review these scriptures that each of the princes mentioned in the Bible is referred to in the masculine. Most of us have made the mistake of assuming these names are simply different names for Satan[vii] . The point here is that they are all referred to in the masculine.

*Canst thou draw out **leviathan** with an hook? or **his** tongue with a cord which thou lettest down?*
—*JOB 41:1*

*It is enough for the disciple that he be as his master, and the servant as his lord. If they have called the master of the house **Beelzebub**, how much more shall they call them of **his** household?* —*MATTHEW 10:25*

*Wherein in time past ye walked according to the course of this world, according to the **prince of the power of the air**, the spirit that now worketh in the children of disobedience:*
—*EPHESIANS 2:2*

*Who is a liar but he that denieth that Jesus is the Christ? **He** is **antichrist**, that denieth the Father and the Son.*
—*1 JOHN 2:22*

*Now is the judgment of this world: now shall the **prince of this world** be cast out.* —*JOHN 12:31*

*Behold now **behemoth**, which I made with thee; **he** eateth grass as an ox.* —*JOB 40:15*

*And the name of the star is called **Wormwood**: and the third part of the waters became wormwood; and many men died of the waters, because they were made bitter.*
—*REVELATION 8:11*

Every evil prince, with the exception of Wormwood, is obviously male in gender. God's Word is so specific. For although the male pronoun is not used for Wormwood, the Holy Spirit deliberately shows this dark angel's gender. The common Greek word for "wormwood" is in fact a feminine word. However, the proper name of the star (angel) that falls to the earth is in the masculine gender. In other words, the Holy Spirit masculinized a female name; this is the exact opposite of the way English boy names like "Paul" are feminized to "Paula" or "Joseph" to "Josephine". Every single dark angel is male.

Finally, we will take a quick look at a passage that has been debated by many through the years.

*That the **sons of God** saw the daughters of men that they were fair; and they took them wives of all which they chose.*
—*GENESIS 6:2*

*Now there was a day when the **sons of God** came to present themselves before the Lord, and Satan came also among them.*
—*JOB 1:6*

The sons of God mentioned in Genesis are fallen angels who came down to earth and mated with the daughters of men. It is crucial that we comprehend the fact that all the angels were created as sons, not daughters and not as bi-sexual beings. Every scripture that alludes to angels supports this premise. So whether the angel is godly or fallen, he is male. There is some form of deception occurring if an angel is appearing as anything other than what he is.

We have heard arguments that it was just because of the male dominated society of biblical times that all the pronouns are masculine. Even if you believe this argument, it does not eliminate all the times the Holy Spirit actually described the angel as a male, or the fact that not one time in scripture is an angel described as a female. The other classes of people mentioned in scripture, such as prophets, pastors,

116

teachers, saints have examples of both male and female members. Yet all angelic verses only use the male gender. So the argument about a male dominated society using masculine pronouns just does not stand up to the test of scripture.

The real question is, "Do you truly believe the scriptures are the inspired Word of God?" We believe that the Holy Spirit inspired every word, not just the thoughts and ideas. If we believe that God has preserved His Word for us today, AND WE DO, then we must accept that the Holy Spirit chose the words He meant to say. He used the male gender when He wanted to designate male. He used the female gender when He wanted to designate female, and He used the neuter gender when He wanted to designate neither male nor female.

It is time to sum up our findings. The Lord left us with no room for doubt. There are a multitude of scriptures that identify the Lord's angels as being male, but there is not even one that suggests that they could be female. There is not even one verse that can be used to justify teaching that female angels exist.

So who are these beings that are masquerading as female angels of the Lord? They are none other than the fallen angels, or as we like to refer to them, dark angels. They are basically fallen male angels who have transformed themselves to appear female. It is an appeal to mankind's senses.

If these female-looking angels are indeed dark angels, then any kind of anointing they bring must be counterfeit. Powerful, even miraculous, but counterfeit. Any manifestations, including miracles and healings, that occur during the ministry of these female-looking angels are demonic. The enemy can heal and deliver by simply removing his own hold or attack on a person. The enemy can move in some very real and powerful giftings. Jesus told us that in the last days we would be inundated with many false signs and wonders. Female angels are just one of them.

For there shall arise false Christs, and false prophets, and shall shew great signs and wonders; insomuch that, if it were possible, they shall deceive the very elect.
—MATTHEW 24:24

Emma is indeed the angel of the prophetic, **the false prophetic!** Jesus said the "very elect" could be deceived by these falsehoods. The "very elect" is not necessarily the general church. It is those who have pressed into the Lord and are hungering for more of

117

Him. The "very elect" are those that have been faithful to intercede for His purposes. The "very elect" are those who have paid the price for moving into the deeper things of God. If this is describing you, the enemy is out to deceive you! It is not our intention to bring condemnation to you or anyone else. This is a warning. It is a stern warning to stay clear of any kind of ministry that is welcoming these fallen angels, innocently or not, into their midst.

The Lord does not try to deceive us, ever. In fact, He teaches us that we must learn to discern between good and evil. Notice that the writer of Hebrews is speaking to the spiritually mature person about exercising his discernment.

> *But strong meat belongeth to them that are of full age, even those who by reason of use have their senses exercised to discern both good and evil.* —HEBREWS 5:14

Do Angel Names Reveal Anything?

Let us move on to other false teachings about angels. Or more appropriately said other indicators that dark angels masquerading as angels of light are among us. In reading through books that give accounts of encounters people have had with angels, some of these angels have very peculiar names. Examples include "Declaration, Independence, Celestial and Constellation," just to name a few. The issue is not necessarily with these particular names, but rather that in the entire Bible, God only tells us the names of two of His angels, Michael and Gabriel. It is fair to say that for angels to give us their names is not a priority or a common biblical practice. That does not mean it will never happen, but it is not a main concern with God or with the angels. Angels are all about bringing worship to God and not about being recognized themselves.

When you read some of these books and see the many unscriptural teachings, you have to wonder how legitimate these names could possibly be. The fact that the individuals are having visitations from female angels should make us highly skeptical of anything they are saying. Notwithstanding that fact, you will find that some of the names given by these angels in these books are just ridiculous. Ridiculous does not make something anti-scriptural. God does do strange things. However, there are some names being reported that are definite evidence of dark angels.

One author says that one of his guardian angels is named "Wonderful", and one of his wife's guardian angels is named "Holy"

118

while yet another one is named "Holy Holy". There is a very serious problem with these three names. Why? They are names of God! "Wonderful" is one of the names of Jesus and "Holy" is one of the names of God.

> *For unto us a child is born, unto us a son is given: and the government shall be upon his shoulder: and his name shall be called **Wonderful**, Counsellor, The mighty God, The everlasting Father, The Prince of Peace.*
>
> —*ISAIAH 9:6*

> *For thus saith the high and lofty One that inhabiteth eternity, **whose name is Holy**; I dwell in the high and holy place, with him also that is of a contrite and humble spirit, to revive the spirit of the humble, and to revive the heart of the contrite ones.* —*ISAIAH 57:15*

The citizens of heaven, you and I, we all cry, "Holy, holy, holy" to God Almighty.

> *And the four beasts had each of them six wings about him; and they were full of eyes within: and they rest not day and night, saying, **Holy, holy, holy, Lord God Almighty**, which was, and is, and is to come.* —*REVELATION 4:8*

God does not share His name or His glory with any one, not even with an angel. Under the Mosaic Law, they did not even fully write out the name of God to prevent profaning it. One of the Ten Commandments says, "*Thou shalt not take the name of the Lord thy God in vain.*" It is incredibly dangerous when we start believing angels who refer to themselves by one of the names of God. This is in direct disobedience to the Ten Commandments.

Wounded Angels?

There is another perverted teaching being propagated by the enemy about the Lord's angels. It is being purported that godly angels can be wounded. In one book, the author reports that he saw an angel sitting on the floor injured. He claims that the Holy Spirit told him that the Lord's angels get injured during spiritual warfare over our cities. The author described a specific "wounded angel position" when these angels come in from a battle.

He goes on to say that the Holy Spirit told him these angels have no place to "go to rest and recuperate." The Lord wanted to know if He could use the author's home as a guesthouse and hospital for His angels. Let us get this straight. The author is saying that the God of all creation who created the heavens and the earth and is the source of all strength, power and glory, has no place of rest for His angels. That is absurd.

Do God's angels need rest? Remember, this author says that the Lord's mighty angels can be wounded. Speaking from my own limited experience in spiritual warfare with the angels, I have yet to see any of the Lord's angels get wounded. I absolutely have seen the enemy hurt and wounded. Do the enemy's forces need a place of rest and recuperation? Yes!

To open your home and heart to minister strength to dark angels masquerading as wounded godly angels is the height of being deceived. "Father, please protect and deliver these ministers and ministries from the deceiver."

Are the Seven Spirits of God Angels?

God is giving incredible revelation about His Seven Spirits. These Seven Spirits are not angels. They represent the seven ways in which God moves and personifies Himself.

A teaching is going around that claims the Seven Spirits come as angels. The person teaching said that one of the Seven Spirits came as a little child. The child was dressed in all white and hooded. The face of the child could not be seen because of the brightness of it. He went on to say that on another occasion one of the Seven Spirits manifested as a woman.

Even though these false teachings may seem harmless to you, understand that they are the net result of the same person who is encountering and ministering with female angels. The enemy can disguise himself in all white and shine with the brightness of God's glory. The enemy can even exude a kind of love that will bring tears to your eyes because of the depth of it. The scriptures say he can transform himself into an angel of light.

It is blasphemy to ascribe Godhood to any other created being. Scriptures say it is the Lamb of God, Jesus Christ our Lord, who has the seven eyes that represent the Seven Spirits. The Seven Spirits are not angels; they are manifestations of God Himself.

*And I beheld, and, lo, in the midst of the throne and of the four beasts, and in the midst of the elders, **stood a Lamb as it had been slain, having seven horns and seven eyes, which are the seven Spirits of God** sent forth into all the earth.*
                                                                        —REVELATION 5:6

Safeguards for Angelic Encounters

Safeguarding angelic encounters is actually a very simple process, if we follow a few rules of engagement based on scripture. The angels of the Lord have some very definite characteristics as shown in scripture.

- Angels will not seek notoriety or personal fanfare.
- Angels will not seek adulation or worship.
- Angels will honor the authority structure into which you have been planted; they will not try to undermine it.
- If an angelic encounter does not align with scripture, assume it is a deception.
- Angels will never change or attempt to disregard the Word of God.
- Apply the litmus test of First John to any angelic encounter. Always ask "Did Jesus Christ come in the flesh?"

Testing the Spirits

We must be very careful with any kind of spiritual visitation we may receive. The Word very simply tells us to test the spirits.

Beloved, believe not every spirit, but <u>try the spirits whether they are of God</u>: because many false prophets are gone out into the world. ²Hereby know ye the Spirit of God: Every spirit that confesseth that Jesus Christ is come in the flesh is of God: ³And <u>every spirit that confesseth not that Jesus Christ is come in the flesh is not of God</u>: and this is that spirit of antichrist, whereof ye have heard that it should come; and even now already is it in the world.   *—1 JOHN 4:1-3*

This is absolutely the safest course to take. Do not risk being deceived. Obey the Word and ask the spirit being that has come to you the question, *"Has Jesus Christ come in the flesh?"* It is interesting that we have yet to read any books or listen to any recorded teachings where this test is even suggested. We cannot be naive or ignorant when dealing in the spirit realm. It is much too dangerous for our souls.

Although we have a book on angels, our focus is on encouraging the saints see God and partner with Him to enter His Kingdom. However, we have always endeavored to make it clear that the most important thing is to know the Lord in an intimate way. In addition, we must be able to operate in the gift of discerning of spirits, and finally we must test the spirits.

We have spent a great deal of time talking about some of the risks of operating in the spirit realm, but our purpose is not to discourage you. You must be seeking God and His Kingdom. The enemy is very busy in his attempt to keep us from entering these eternal realms. He is doing his best to cast a bad light on those who would take steps of faith to access the Kingdom of God. Truthfully, the spirit realm can be the safest place for you to be when you are properly submitted to your God-given authority and when you are operating according to scripture.

Be wary of those who hype up or boast of their encounters in heaven or the spirit realm. Be cautious of those that make a big deal of particular angels and announce that certain angels will be present in their services. Make sure that the glory is going to God and that no undue attention is being placed on the angelic. Angels are not attention seekers. They serve God and partner with us to see God's Kingdom come and His purposes come forth.

The greatest safeguard is in knowing God's Word and making sure everything lines up with it. Humility is definitely a characteristic of the true servant of God. Beware of false humility.

The best way to hone and refine your discernment is by praying in the Spirit. That is right, intercession. The more you know the Lord, His voice and His presence, the less likely you are to be deceived by a counterfeit. Always remember, the enemy ultimately has to abscond with God's glory to empower his kingdom. All power on earth and in heaven belongs to God. The enemy is in the business of stealing anointings and giftings, and he desires to inhabit places of resident glory. The enemy confiscates and uses this glory and these giftings for his own purposes.

Through intercession God will teach you more about His Kingdom and how the kingdom of darkness works. The Lord taught me to battle evil angels in the second heavens long before I encountered them here on this earth. This familiarity of the forces and strategies of the enemy came as I pursued the Lord through intercession. As strange as it was when God began teaching me about the dark realm, I am so grateful that He took the time to do it because my chances of being deceived have been greatly reduced.

We do not believe that the individuals who have been deceived and are sharing their revelations are evil. If the "very elect" can be deceived, that means it could happen to any of us. My prayer is that God will open their eyes to the truth. When the Lord does that, He will bring them back into alignment with the purposes for which they were created.

We pray for you, too. We pray that your eyes would be opened to the truth of God's Word and that God will increase your discernment. We also pray that He will give you a passion for prayer and seeking His heart. We are living in the most incredible time in the history of mankind. As saints, we have amazing assignments that have been given to us by our Father. The Father is releasing His angels to help us carry out His purposes. We need to get busy for our King, and lay aside these things that would so easily beset us.

Unequally Yoked

God does not partner with the enemy in ministry. The Lord's angels will not minister alongside a fallen angel. When scripture speaks of being "unequally yoked" it is not just referring to marriage. Two other scriptures even more pointedly address this issue of cooperating where demons are involved.

But I say, that the things which the Gentiles sacrifice, they sacrifice to devils, and not to God: and I would not that ye should have fellowship with devils.
—1 CORINTHIANS 10:20

Be ye not unequally yoked together with unbelievers: for what fellowship hath righteousness with unrighteousness? and what communion hath light with darkness?
—2 CORINTHIANS 6:14

The word "fellowship" in 1 Corinthians 10 speaks of partnership. The enemy does not intentionally try to fulfill the righteousness or purpose of God. In fact, he specifically tries to defeat it. It was never God's intention for us to partner with the enemy in any fashion.

The challenge for many believers is that these dark angels are very alluring and powerful. Often when they come, they activate the visionary capacity of an individual to see things in the spirit realm. If a person has not or does not normally see things in the spirit, this can be a very exciting experience. These fallen angels can come with very accurate prophetic words and insightful revelations.

Several of the authors and ministers that have been exposed to these fallen angels are declaring revelations of heaven and the angelic ministry that are perverted. Some of the descriptions we have heard of heaven and the Throne are not supported by scripture. Any revelations being released by individuals involved with these types of angels should be questioned and scrutinized carefully.

What should you do if you are in a meeting and Emma is welcomed in? First, realize that the authority was just relinquished to the demonic realm. We just read that we are not to have fellowship with unrighteousness or communion with darkness. Whatever you decide to do, remember to be gracious and do not make a scene.

Could God have you stay and pray in the Spirit for the protection of everyone else? Yes, but you had better know that is what God has asked you to do. And do not forget, whatever you do must be done very quietly and humbly. You are not the one in authority, nor are you the one who will have to give an answer to God. Be wise and proceed with caution.

Several people concerned about the books, CDs and videos connected with these authors and ministries have asked what they should do with them. You will have to seek the Lord for this answer. Some of the ministries involved have blessed us greatly over the years. For our church and ourselves, we have had to make some difficult decisions. God will speak to your heart and give you the wisdom and discernment required to make your decision.

[vii] Pastor Ron Crawford, in his book, *Princes of the Dark Realm*, describes at length Satan and the seven princes of the dark realm that work with him to wreak havoc on this world.

8

Encounters with Heavenly Believers

Paul came home one day and told me that during prayer he had been approached in the spirit by the prophet Samuel. He said that Samuel spoke of the Kingdom of God, words right out of the scriptures. Although the encounter was fairly short, Samuel was encouraging and instructed him in the ways of God. Then Samuel left.

I was both encouraged myself and troubled. Encouraged, because there is nothing like receiving a message directly from the heart of Father God; often this has happened in prayer, sometimes directly from the lips of God Himself and sometimes from the lips of an angel. Troubled, because this time the messenger was not an angel, but a saint that scripture says has already passed from this physical sphere into eternity.

The scriptures are our authoritative rule of faith and conduct, and all areas of our lives including spiritual experience must be judged by the Word. So every spiritual encounter, every spiritual experience must align with the Word of God. I immediately questioned an interaction with a "heavenly saint" based on my memory of scripture. I recalled a verse in Deuteronomy about necromancy and a story recorded in 1 Samuel 28 between King Saul and the woman with a familiar spirit who called up Samuel from the dead. When faced with new spiritual experiences, we need to imitate the Bereans of Acts 17 who *"received the word with all readiness of mind, and searched the scriptures daily, whether those things were so"*. So began a journey through scripture to discover what God really says about such experiences. Could encounters with heaven-dwelling saints be of God, or was this some deception of our enemy?

What is a Necromancer?

One thing we have learned in studying scripture is that we must *"rightly divide the word of truth."* One aspect of "rightly" is to align with God's righteous ways, not with man's often-biased interpretation. Since childhood, we had both assumed that any interaction with a dead person was actually an interaction with a demon disguised as the dead person. This assumption was not specifically based in scripture; it just "made sense". Unfortunately, logic is often the church's measure of truth instead of the actual Word of God.

In Isaiah 55:8 it says, *"For my thoughts are not your thoughts, neither are your ways my ways, saith the LORD."* Just because something "makes sense" does not mean it is right or that it aligns with the truth. So we first began with the word "necromancer" in Deuteronomy 18 where the law forbids divination and all sorts of evil spiritual practices.

> When thou art come into the land which the Lord thy God giveth thee, thou shalt not learn to do after the abominations of those nations. *[10]There shall not be found among you any one that maketh his son or his daughter to pass through the fire, or that useth divination, or an observer of times, or an enchanter, or a witch, 11Or a charmer, or a consulter with familiar spirits, or a wizard, or a necromancer. [12]For all that do these things are an abomination unto the Lord: and because of these abominations the Lord thy God doth drive them out from before thee. [13]Thou shalt be perfect with the Lord thy God. [14]For these nations, which thou shalt possess, hearkened unto observers of times, and unto diviners: but as for thee, the Lord thy God hath not suffered thee so to do.*
> —DEUTERONOMY 18:9-14

The word necromancer is actually the combination of two Hebrew words, *"darash"* which means to seek with care or with the intent to know. For example, David *darash* about Bathsheba to find out who she was with the intent of getting to know her (2 Samuel 11:3). The word connotes an inquiry after knowledge, advice or insight into a particular problem as when Rebekah "went to inquire of the Lord" about the twins struggling within her womb (Genesis 25:22). This inquiry could be made through a divine spokesman as when the people came to Moses to inquire of the Lord (Exodus18:15) or when King Zedekiah asked Jeremiah to inquire of the Lord (Jeremiah 21:2). Finally, the word is used to seek the word of a false deity, often involving the use of complex rituals (Ezekiel 21:21). This "inquiring" of false gods was forbidden by the law (Deut. 12:30).

You will notice that one involved in practicing necromancy is seeking communication with the dead with the intent to find out something. This is what King Saul was doing when he went to the woman with a familiar spirit asking her to call up Samuel so he could find out what he should do (1 Samuel 28:7-25).

Inquiry or seeking is by definition an active pursuit, or a conscious choice to go after something or someone. When you are praying and seeking God and not an interaction with anyone, then you are not seeking to commune with the dead. Paul had not been seeking this type of experience and in fact was surprised by it. So he was not inquiring.

The second part of the word necromancer is *"muwth"* which means to die or to kill. According to the Theological Wordbook of the Old Testament (TWOT), *muwth "may refer to death by natural causes or to violent death. The root is not limited to the death of humans, although it is used predominantly that way. This is a universally used Semitic root for dying and death. The Canaanites employed it as the name of the god of death and the netherworld, Mot (cf. ANET, pp. 138-42)".*

So necromancy involves seeking to inquire **of the dead**. This may sound silly, but to understand this scripture we must understand what "dead" means.

What is Death?

Biblically there are two types of death. One is physical death in which our bodies die. We cease to live in the physical frame or in the flesh. Our bodies begin the decaying process of returning to the dust from which we were created. This is known as physical death.

The second death is spiritual death in which our spirits are not indwelt by the living Son of God. Before salvation we are "dead in our trespasses and sins". If we do not accept Jesus Christ as Lord before our physical death, this spiritual death becomes permanent and we will dwell forever in a place of everlasting torment.

As there are two types of death, there are also two types of life. One is the life of the body which every human being experiences during the period of their residence on earth. The second is the life of the spirit, which those who have accepted Christ Jesus as Lord may enjoy both now and for all eternity.

Finally, there are two types of bodies. One is our physical body made of flesh and blood. After the death of our physical body, those who have spiritual life in Christ receive a new body. This eternal, incorruptible body is one in which we will dwell forever with God in eternity. Scripture says that our corruptible physical body which "dies" on earth will be swallowed up by our incorruptible eternal body which will never die.

Blessed and holy is he that hath part in the first resurrection: on such the second death hath no power, but they shall be priests of God and of Christ, and shall reign with him a thousand years. —Revelation 20:6

For this corruptible must put on incorruption, and this mortal must put on immortality. [54]*So when this corruptible shall have put on incorruption, and this mortal shall have put on immortality, then shall be brought to pass the saying that is written, Death is swallowed up in victory.* —1 CORINTHIANS 15:53-54

For the saint of God who has experienced physical death, there is no second death. They move from death to life. Their corruptible physical body is replaced with an incorruptible, eternal body. They are not "dead" in either the physical or spiritual sense of the word. If fact they are more alive than those of us who are still dwelling in our physical body on the earth, for we are still subject to the "first death" or the death of our physical bodies. When we accept Jesus as Savior and Lord, we receive eternal life only in our spirits, but our bodies are still subject to physical death. When we leave our mortal, physical bodies, we have only life. Paul the Apostle said in Philippians 1:21-22, *"For to me to live is Christ, and to die is gain."* What was that "gain"? It was living with Christ in an eternal body, always present with the Lord.

Verily, verily, I say unto you, He that heareth my word, and <u>believeth on him that sent me, hath everlasting life</u>, and shall not come into condemnation; but is passed from death unto life. —JOHN 5:24

For the <u>wages of sin is death; but the gift of God is eternal life</u> through Jesus Christ our Lord.

—ROMANS 6:23

For <u>the law of the Spirit of life in Christ Jesus hath made me free from the law of sin and death</u>

—ROMANS 8:2

According to the Word of God, the saints of God have passed from death unto life. **They are not "dead".**

Verily, verily, I say unto you, He that heareth my word, and believeth on him that sent me, hath everlasting life, and shall not come into condemnation; but <u>is passed from death unto life</u>. —JOHN 5:24

We know that <u>we have passed from death unto life</u>, because we love the brethren. He that loveth not his brother abideth in death. —1 JOHN 3:14

But they which shall be accounted worthy to obtain that world, and the resurrection from the dead, neither marry, nor are given in marriage: [36]Neither can they die any more: for they are equal unto the angels; and are the children of God, being the children of the resurrection.

—LUKE 20:35-36

Those individuals who lived on this earth and passed from this earth before the death and resurrection of Jesus Christ our Lord and Savior were held in a place Jesus called "Abraham's bosom" or paradise. Upon Jesus' resurrection, He "led captivity, captive", releasing them from the realms of Satan's domain and leading them into their eternal home with God.

And it came to pass, that the beggar died, and was carried by the angels into Abraham's bosom: the rich man also died, and was buried; ²³And in hell he lift up his eyes, being in torments, and seeth Abraham afar off, and Lazarus in his bosom.
—LUKE 16:22-23

Wherefore he saith, When he ascended up on high, he led captivity captive, and gave gifts unto men.
—EPHESIANS 4:8

And, behold, the veil of the temple was rent in twain from the top to the bottom; and the earth did quake, and the rocks rent; ⁵²And the graves were opened; and many bodies of the saints which slept arose, ⁵³And came out of the graves after his resurrection, and went into the holy city, and appeared unto many.
—MATTHEW 27:51-53

The chart below shows these four states of being that we have just discussed. **The only state that can truly be considered fully alive is where an individual is saved and already dwelling in an immortal body. The very word immortal means "cannot die".**

Spiritually Alive	Spiritually Dead
Saved, in mortal body	*Lost, in mortal body*
Saved, in immortal body	*Lost, in tormented body*

Without question, the scriptures teach that those who have gone to be with the Lord are not dead. So an encounter with a heavenly saint like Samuel cannot, by definition, be necromancy.

Are Encounters Scriptural?

Although it was good to know that the experience Paul had was not necromancy, there was still the question of the rightness of encounters of this nature. Although Paul did not speak of this encounter to others, not long after his first experience, other members of our congregation began telling of similar encounters. Paul had additional encounters and our Senior Pastor began to speak of encounters he had experienced with heavenly believers as well.

We will use the term "heavenly believers" to indicate those individuals who have died in the physical sense and are now living in heaven with the Lord. Patriarchs from the pages of the Old Testament like Abraham, Moses and David would fit this description. Apostles and believers from the New Testament like Paul, John and Peter would also fit this description. Finally, any believer that has passed from death unto life whether they were famous men of God from ages past or anonymous saints known only to the Lord, all would bear the title "heavenly believer".

So the question became not "Is this necromancy?", but "Is this of God?" Does scripture give evidence of this type of encounter? The answer we found was a resounding YES. As we began to search the scriptures, we discovered more and more verses about these types of experiences. We began to see a pattern, yet before my study they had been so subtle and so understated that we had passed right over them. As we continue to study, my prayer is that God would open our eyes to see what the scriptures actually say and that we are not blinded by what we have always assumed they meant. Let us not be like the two men on the road to Emmaus who knew Jesus was dead, so they assumed that the one walking with them could not be Jesus. Jesus opened their eyes. Our prayer is that the Holy Spirit will open the eyes of our understanding as well that we too might see what God has said in the scriptures.

Then opened he their understanding, that they might understand the scriptures, —LUKE 24:45

Before we explore the less obvious scriptural references, let us look first at the life of Jesus, Himself. Scriptures teach that we are to be like Jesus. We are to walk the way He walked and live our lives after the pattern of His life. Jesus encountered heavenly believers. Before you argue that Jesus is different because He is God, and before you assume His experience with heavenly believers is not evidence that these encounters are meant for humans, let us look at what the scripture says.

The Bible teaches that when Jesus came to die for our sins, He laid aside His divine abilities and lived His life using only the power of prayer to which each human being has access. Hebrews 4:15 says, *"For we have not an high priest which cannot be touched with the feeling of our infirmities; but was in all points tempted like as we are, yet without sin."* It also prophesies, commands and encourages us to be like Jesus.

For even hereunto were ye called: because Christ also suffered for us, leaving us an example, that <u>ye should follow his steps</u>: —*1 PETER 2:21*

Verily, verily, I say unto you, <u>He that believeth on me, the works that I do shall he do also; and greater works than these shall he do; because I go unto my Father.</u> —*JOHN 14:12*

Consider this simple list of the things that Jesus did and scriptures that teach we are to do these same things. Jesus

- Obeyed His Father God's will

And he went a little farther, and fell on his face, and prayed, saying, O my Father, if it be possible, let this cup pass from me: <u>nevertheless not as I will, but as thou wilt.</u> — *MATTHEW 26:39*

And he said unto them, When ye pray, say, Our Father which art in heaven, Hallowed be thy name. Thy kingdom come. <u>Thy will be done</u>, as in heaven, so in earth. —*LUKE 11:2*

- Preached the gospel

*From that time <u>Jesus began to **preach**</u>, and to say, Repent: for the kingdom of heaven is at hand.* — *MATTHEW 4:17*

And he said unto them, <u>Go ye into all the world, and preach the gospel to every creature.</u> —*MARK 16:15*

- Healed the sick, cast out demons, raised the dead

And these signs shall follow them that believe; <u>In my name shall they cast out devils</u>; they shall speak with new tongues; 18They shall take up serpents; and if they drink any deadly thing, it shall not hurt them; <u>they shall lay hands on the sick, and they shall recover</u>.
—MARK 16:17-18

<u>Heal the sick, cleanse the lepers, raise the dead, cast out devils</u>: freely ye have received, freely give.
—MATTHEW 10:8

- Suffered persecution

Remember the word that I said unto you, The servant is not greater than his lord. <u>If they have persecuted me, they will also persecute you</u>; if they have kept my saying, they will keep yours also. —JOHN 15:20

- Took up His cross

*And Pilate wrote a title, and <u>put it on the **cross**.</u> And the writing was, JESUS OF NAZARETH THE KING OF THE JEWS.* —JOHN 19:19

Then said Jesus unto his disciples, If any man will come after me<u>, let him deny himself, and take up his cross, and follow me</u>. —MATTHEW 16:24

- Laid down His life

As the Father knoweth me, even so know I the Father: and <u>I lay down my life</u> for the sheep. —JOHN 10:15

Hereby perceive we the love of God, because <u>he laid down his life for us: and we ought to lay down our lives for the brethren</u>. —1 JOHN 3:16

- Is dressed in the white linen of the saints in the spirit realm

And was transfigured before them: and his face did shine as the sun, <u>and his raiment was white as the light</u>.
—MATTHEW 17:2

133

And to her was granted that she should be arrayed in fine linen, clean and white: for the fine linen is the righteousness of saints. —REVELATION 19:8

- Was resurrected from the dead

And declared to be the Son of God with power, according to the spirit of holiness, by the resurrection from the dead: —ROMANS 1:4

For if we have been planted together in the likeness of his death, we shall be also in the likeness of his resurrection: —ROMANS 6:5

- Spends His time now in intercession

Wherefore he is able also to save them to the uttermost that come unto God by him, seeing he ever liveth to make intercession for them. —HEBREWS 7:25

I exhort therefore, that, first of all, supplications, prayers, intercessions, and giving of thanks, be made for all men; —1 TIMOTHY 2:1

- Encountered heaven-dwelling saints and took His disciples with Him to share the encounter

And after six days Jesus taketh with him Peter, and James, and John, and leadeth them up into an high mountain apart by themselves: and he was transfigured before them. 3And his raiment became shining, exceeding white as snow; so as no fuller on earth can white them. ⁴And there appeared unto them Elias with Moses: and they were talking with Jesus. — MARK 9:2-4

This list is of necessity shortened and leaves out many other aspects of Jesus' life and the many things that He did. In fact, John says the Bible itself leaves out many things that Jesus did.

And there are also many other things which Jesus did, the which, if they should be written every one, I suppose that even the world itself could not contain the books that should be written. Amen. — JOHN 21:25

However, if you study this topic, you will find that there is much more evidence to support the idea that in every way and in every experience we are to be like Jesus than there is to support the idea that in all but this one area we are to follow Jesus. We do not claim this is conclusive proof that encounters with heaven-dwelling saints are of God, but it is one more bit of evidence we must consider.

The Transfiguration

Let us look more closely at this encounter between Jesus and heaven-dwelling believers. It is one of the most famous events in Jesus' life. It is one that is celebrated in art, preached from pulpits, and generally held up as a defining moment in His ministry. Matthew, Mark, Luke, John and 2 Peter all tell about Jesus' transfiguration in which Moses and Elijah are sent to strengthen Him for His upcoming trial and crucifixion (Matthew 17:1-13; Mark 9:2-13; Luke 9:28-36; John 1:14; 2 Peter 1:16-18). We have quoted here only from Mark, but the other accounts reflect the same events.

> *And after six days <u>Jesus taketh with him Peter, and James, and John</u>, and leadeth them up into an high mountain apart by themselves: and he was transfigured before them. [3]And his raiment became shining, exceeding white as snow; so as no fuller on earth can white them. [4]And there appeared unto them Elias with Moses: and they were talking with Jesus. [5]And Peter answered and said to Jesus, Master, it is good for us to be here: and let us make three tabernacles; one for thee, and one for Moses, and one for Elias. [6]For he wist not what to say; for they were sore afraid. [7]And there was a cloud that overshadowed them: and a voice came out of the cloud, saying, This is my beloved Son: hear him. [8]And suddenly, when they had looked round about, they saw no man any more, save Jesus only with themselves.* —MARK 9:2-8

There is much to be learned from this incident. First, notice that Jesus takes His three closest disciples with Him to the mount. With the exception of His passion week, every other instance of Jesus going up to a mount to pray was alone. He did "sit on the mount" to teach the multitudes, but this was a far different behavior than going to the mountain for the purpose of communing with His Father. Matthew 14:23, Mark 6:46 and John 6:15 all tell of Jesus going alone to a mountain to pray while His disciples cross the sea in a boat. Luke 6:12

specifically says Jesus went to the mountain and the next morning called His disciples and chose the twelve. Yet on this occasion, Jesus takes Peter, James and John with Him to the mountain, leaving the other nine waiting at the bottom.

Jesus spent His teaching focus while on the earth instilling into His disciples exactly how to live. He lived the spiritual walk in front of them that He wanted them to follow. He taught them how to live, to pray, to minister, to suffer persecution, and to die. **We believe He took these three up on to the mount to witness how to interact with the spirit realm.** You will remember that Peter immediately responds with a desire to worship Moses and Elijah. This is a desire that Jesus wanted to reveal and eliminate so that in the future when this type of encounter occurred, Peter's wrong response would not be followed.

If you think about the church through history, one of its greatest errors has been the worship of those who are near to the Lord instead of worship of the Lord Himself. This encounter in the company of the disciples gave the opportunity for the Lord Jesus Christ to teach the disciples one more aspect of following Him.

When they reach the top, Jesus is transfigured. The Greek word for transfigured will be familiar. It is *"metamorphoo"* from which we get the English word *"metamorphosis"*. It literally means to be changed from one form to another. The interesting thing about this event is that Jesus was showing His disciples His own spiritual body. He was showing them the white linen with which He is clothed in the spirit realm. You will note that Jesus is still in His physical body. He has not yet experienced physical death, and He has not yet received His eternal body. According to Jesus' own words to Mary after His resurrection He was not yet in His eternal body because He commands Mary not to touch Him for that very reason. Later that same day that Mary saw Him, He has ascended and received His eternal body and instructs His disciples to *"handle me and see"*.

Jesus saith unto her, <u>Touch me not; for I am not yet ascended to my Father:</u> but go to my brethren, and say unto them, I ascend unto my Father, and your Father; and to my God, and your God. —JOHN 20:17

<u>Behold my hands and my feet, that it is I myself: handle me, and see;</u> for a spirit hath not flesh and bones, as ye see me have. —LUKE 24:39

So when Jesus is "transfigured" before Peter, James and John, He is showing them what He looks like in the spirit realm. Each of us is a spirit, and we all have spiritual bodies. A saying that is popular in the church today expresses this best, "We are spirit beings, given an eternal soul, enduring a temporary physical condition."

It is sown a natural body; it is raised a spiritual body. There is a natural body, and there is a spiritual body.
—1 CORINTHIANS 15:44

So *"metamorphoo"* applied to Jesus taking on or changing into His spiritual body. This is a very orthodox doctrine believed throughout the church today. The word *"metamorphoo"* is only used four times in scripture. Two times it is translated "transfigured" and refers directly to Jesus' own transfiguration. The remaining two times it is translated "transformed" and "changed". Both of these uses are direct commands to believers to be *"metamorphoo"*. We are also to walk and talk in our spiritual bodies, not just our physical bodies.

*And be not conformed to this world: but be ye **transformed** by the renewing of your mind, that ye may prove what is that good, and acceptable, and perfect, will of God.*
—ROMANS 12:2

*But we all, with open face beholding as in a glass the glory of the Lord, are **changed** into the same image from glory to glory, even as by the Spirit of the Lord.*
—2 CORINTHIANS 3:18

So Jesus was not only demonstrating how to handle encounters with heaven-dwelling believers to His disciples, He was at the same time demonstrating that they, too, are to enter into this *"transformation"*.

Visits in Jerusalem

Scriptures say that every word will be established in the mouth of two or three witnesses. So we will look at other examples of heavenly believers interacting with men on the earth.

And the graves were opened; and <u>many bodies of the saints which slept arose</u>, [53]And came out of the graves after his resurrection, and went into the holy city, and <u>appeared unto many</u>.
—MATTHEW 27:52-53

At the Ascension – The "Aner"

Scriptures tell us that two men appeared to the disciples at the ascension. The question is, "Were they men or angels?" Scholars and Bible commentators differ on this point. Many just "assume" they were angels without any exegetical explanation. Others simply say they could have been humans or angels. The scripture does not say they were angels. In fact it specifically recognizes them as men, both in the Greek and the English. We realize this does not prove they were heavenly believers. However, the church world has jumped to the conclusion that they had to be angels, because it fits man's theology when the internal evidence would suggest a different conclusion.

First of all, it is the saints who wear white according to scriptures. Second, the disciples standing around do not react with fear the way they do when they see angels (Matthew 1:20; Matthew 28:5; Luke 1:13; Luke 1:30; Luke 2:10).

In fact, the scripture says these two men "stood by". They were not suspended in the clouds as so many paintings of the resurrection depict. Finally, these two are dressed just like Moses and Elijah were on the mount of Transfiguration and speak to Jesus of Him fulfilling His full work which we know includes His death, resurrection, ascension and return. This is a strikingly similar topic to the one that Moses and Elijah discussed with Jesus on the mount of Transfiguration.

And while they looked stedfastly toward heaven as he went up, behold, <u>two men stood by them in white apparel;</u> [11] Which also said, Ye men of Galilee, why stand ye gazing up into heaven? this same Jesus, which is taken up from you into heaven, shall so come in like manner as ye have seen him go into heaven.
—ACTS 1:10-11

In both the Luke and Acts passages that describe this event, the Greek word for "men" is *aner*. Of the 170 uses of this word in the New Testament, 166 specifically refer to a "human" and not an angel. This is the word used for Moses and Elijah on the mount of Transfiguration and for a host of other men mentioned specifically by name or circumstance.

The remaining four verses are all in question as to whether they are men or angels. In all four instances, the English translators choose the word "man or men" and the theologians differ. Many commentators choose to assume these verses really meant "angels", although the Holy Spirit used the word for men. Other commentators write that these verses are speaking of men.

Two of these verses are found in the lives of Cornelius and Paul. Cornelius says he saw a man. Cornelius' servant in speaking to Peter says Cornelius saw an angel. Paul said he saw a man in a vision.

And Cornelius said, Four days ago I was fasting until this hour; and at the ninth hour I prayed in my house, and, behold, <u>a man stood before me in bright clothing,</u>

—ACTS 10:30

And a vision appeared to Paul in the night; There stood <u>a man of Macedonia</u>, and prayed him, saying, Come over into Macedonia, and help us.   *—ACTS 16:9*

The remaining two verses are the ones at Jesus ascension that we are considering, Acts 1:10-11 and Luke 24:4.

Another way to look at this linguistic question is to look at the words the Holy Spirit used when we know absolutely the scriptures are referring to an angel. In this situation, the Holy Spirit used another Greek word *"aggelos"*, which actually means a messenger. Of the 180 uses of the word *aggelos*, 173 are translated angel(s,'s) and only seven refer to human messengers, like John the Baptist. Here again the English translators used the word "angel" when scripture indicated an angel and the word "messenger" when the context indicated a human.

So there is a distinct likelihood that more than 500 disciples at the ascension encountered heavenly believers. We must also consider that Cornelius probably encountered a heavenly believer, not an angel.

Paul the Apostle

Not only did Paul encounter the "man of Macedonia", but in his second letter to the Corinthians, the Apostle Paul describes an encounter he had with another man that very possibly is a heavenly believer. Paul specifically says the encounter happened in a vision, which precludes it from being someone who just came and talked to Paul in the natural. Paul also specifically states that this man he encountered had been caught up to the third heaven. Whether the man referred to was still in his physical body or not, Paul believed the man had been into heaven, and we know that heavenly believers dwell in heaven. So either Paul himself encountered a heavenly believer, or the man he met in a vision encountered heavenly believers. Either way, this is an example of the situations for which we are searching the scriptures.

It is not expedient for me doubtless to glory. I will come to visions and revelations of the Lord. ²I knew a man in Christ above fourteen years ago, (whether in the body, I cannot tell; or whether out of the body, I cannot tell: God knoweth;) such an one caught up to the third heaven. ³And I knew such a man, (whether in the body, or out of the body, I cannot tell: God knoweth;) ⁴How that he was caught up into paradise, and heard unspeakable words, which it is not lawful for a man to utter. —2 CORINTHIANS 12:1-4

John the Revelator

The Apostle John is taken to heaven and encounters heavenly believers there.

After this I looked, and, behold, a door was opened in heaven: and the first voice which I heard was as it were of a trumpet talking with me; which said, Come up hither, and I will shew thee things which must be hereafter. ²And immediately <u>I was in the spirit: and, behold, a throne was set in heaven, and one sat on the throne.</u> —Revelation 4:1-2

And after these things <u>I heard a great voice of much people in heaven</u>, saying, Alleluia; Salvation, and glory, and honour, and power, unto the Lord our God: —REVELATION 19:1

Daniel

Daniel, in the midst of a vision, listens in on a conversation between two heavenly believers who are discussing the meaning of the vision and then later hears a heavenly believer instruct Gabriel to make Daniel to understand the meaning of the vision. Like we discussed before, the word used for "man" means a human, not just a being. Also the word for "saint" here means someone who is purified. God's angels did not sin and do not need "purification".

[1]In the third year of the reign of king Belshazzar a vision appeared unto me, even unto me Daniel, after that which appeared unto me at the first. . . .[13]Then I heard one saint [literally means one who has been purified or sanctified] speaking, and another saint said unto that certain saint which spake, How long shall be the vision concerning the daily sacrifice, and the transgression of desolation, to give both the sanctuary and the host to be trodden under foot? . . .[15]And it came to pass, when I, even I Daniel, had seen the vision, and sought for the meaning, then, behold, there stood before me as the appearance of a man [literally appearance of a warrior]. [16]And I heard a man's [literally "adam" – a human] voice between the banks of Ulai, which called, and said, Gabriel, make this man to understand the vision.
—DANIEL 8:1, 13, 15-16

Great Cloud of Witnesses

We love to quote the scripture, but do we really believe we are surrounded by heavenly believers? The exact wording says a cloud of *marturia* or "martyrs". The scriptures say we are surrounded. In fact, the word for "compassed about" literally means something that is bound to us, like the millstone that should be hanged about the neck of one who offends a little one (Mark 9:42, Luke 17:2).

And these all, having obtained a good report through faith, received not the promise: [40]God having provided some better thing for us, that they without us should not be made perfect. [12:1]Wherefore seeing we also are compassed about with so great a cloud of witnesses, let us lay aside every weight, and the sin which doth so easily beset us, and let us run with patience the race that is set before us, [2]Looking unto Jesus the author and finisher of our faith; who for the joy that was set before him endured the cross, despising the shame, and is set down at the right hand of the throne of God.
—HEBREWS 11:39-12:2

Man with the Inkhorn

Ezekiel tells of a vision in which six men are called by the Lord to administer judgment. The word for "men" here is *"enowsh"*

141

the word for "mortal", and comes from the root word *"anash"* which means to be frail or feeble. It is used 516 times in the Old Testament, always translated as human (man, men, servant, etc.). Again, theology assumes based on the activity of these individuals that they are angels, and they could be. However, the Holy Spirit again used a word that in every other place in scripture truly means a human.

> *And, behold, six __men__ came from the way of the higher gate, which lieth toward the north, and every man a slaughter weapon in his hand; and one man among them was clothed with linen, with a writer's inkhorn by his side: and they went in, and stood beside the brasen altar.*
> *—EZEKIEL 9:2*

Watchers and Holy Ones

Daniel tells of another vision in which he specifically encounters heavenly believers. This particular example should be noted carefully, because in the same context Daniel saw and could distinguish between the heavenly believer (holy one) and an angel (watcher). Hebrew scholars even agree on this translation of the words used.

> *I saw in the visions of my head upon my bed, and, behold, a watcher and an holy one came down from heaven;*
> *—DANIEL 4:13*

> *This matter is by the decree of the watchers, and the demand by the word of the holy ones: to the intent that the living may know that the most High ruleth in the kingdom of men, and giveth it to whomsoever he will, and setteth up over it the basest of men.*
> *—DANIEL 4:17*

> *And whereas the king saw a watcher and an holy one coming down from heaven, and saying, Hew the tree down, and destroy it; yet leave the stump of the roots thereof in the earth, even with a band of iron and brass, in the tender grass of the field; and let it be wet with the dew of heaven, and let his portion be with the beasts of the field, till seven times pass over him;*
> *—DANIEL 4:23*

Jesus is King of Saints

Jesus is fully God, but He is also fully man. He is Himself a "heavenly believer" with a heavenly body as we saw in the resurrection and ascension verses cited earlier. So when He shows Himself to the men on the Emmaus road, the disciples during the 40 days before His ascension and later Paul on the Damascus road, not to mention the thousands of people who have seen Him down through the ages, He is encountering them as a heavenly believer. He is encountering them as one who once lived in a physical body on the earth and now dwells in an eternal body in heaven.

Melchisedek

Could Melchisedek be a heavenly believer? He is obviously not an angel, because he is a priest and angels cannot be priests. And the scripture says he lives forever, just like heavenly believers. This is a possibility, but before we can truly use this example, the Lord will have to open our understanding to the phrase in the middle of the passage about Melchisedek not having a "beginning of days". We offer it here only to be thorough.

> *For this Melchisedec, king of Salem, <u>priest of the most high God</u>, who met Abraham returning from the slaughter of the kings, and blessed him; ... [3]Without father, without mother, without descent, having neither beginning of days, nor end of life; but <u>made like unto the Son of God</u>; abideth a priest continually. [4]Now consider how great <u>this man was</u>, unto whom even the patriarch Abraham gave the tenth of the spoils.*
> *—HEBREWS 7:1, 3-4*

Enoch

Jude says that Enoch is coming with 10,000 saints to execute judgment on the ungodly. The context is of the battle at Jesus' second coming that ushers in the millennial reign of Christ. This sounds like big time encounters between humans on earth and heavenly believers. John the Revelator also makes mention of these encounters.

And Enoch also, the seventh from Adam, prophesied of these, saying, Behold, <u>the Lord cometh with ten thousands of his saints,</u> ¹⁵To execute judgment upon all, and to convince all that are ungodly among them of all their ungodly deeds which they have ungodly committed, and of all their hard speeches which ungodly sinners have spoken against him.

—JUDE 1:14-15

And I saw heaven opened, and behold a white horse; and he that sat upon him was called Faithful and True, and in righteousness he doth judge and make war. ... ¹⁴And <u>the armies which were in heaven followed him upon white horses, clothed in fine linen, white and clean.</u>

—REVELATION 19:11, 14

Sitting Down in the Kingdom of Heaven

Does Jesus refer to this type of interaction when He speaks of us sitting down with heavenly believers in the Kingdom of Heaven? What and where is the Kingdom of Heaven?

When Jesus heard it, he marvelled, and said to them that followed, Verily I say unto you, I have not found so great faith, no, not in Israel. ¹¹And I say unto you, That <u>many shall come from the east and west, and shall sit down [anaklino] with Abraham, and Isaac, and Jacob, in the kingdom of heaven</u> . ¹²But the children of the kingdom shall be cast out into outer darkness: there shall be weeping and gnashing of teeth.

—MATTHEW 8:10-12

The Greek word for "sit down" is *anaklino* and is used frequently throughout the New Testament. All uses are in the present tense indicating that the "sitting down" was happening right then, as the event was unfolding. For example, when Jesus sat down in the publican's house or when Jesus commanded everyone to sit down before the miracle of the loaves and fishes.

And it came to pass, as Jesus sat at meat in the house, behold, many publicans and sinners <u>came and sat down with him and his disciples.</u>   *—MATTHEW 9:10*

*And he commanded the <u>multitude to sit down on the grass, and
took the five loaves, and the two fishes</u>, and looking up to
heaven, he blessed, and brake, and gave the loaves to his
disciples, and the disciples to the multitude.*
— MATTHEW 14:19

The term "Kingdom of Heaven" is only used in Matthew. In
most of these verses, it is apparent that the Kingdom already exists and
we are to step into it. We are expected to be entering into and living
within the Kingdom of Heaven on a daily basis, now.

*From that time Jesus began to preach, and to say, <u>Repent: for
the kingdom of heaven is at hand. [approaching]</u>*
—MATTHEW 4:17

*Blessed are the poor in spirit: <u>for theirs is the kingdom of
heaven.</u> [is = present tense versus will be = future tense]*
—MATTHEW 5:3

*Blessed are they which are persecuted for righteousness' sake:
<u>for theirs is the kingdom of heaven.</u>[is = present tense versus
will be = future tense]*   —MATTHEW 5:10

*For I say unto you, That except your righteousness shall
exceed the righteousness of the scribes and Pharisees, ye shall
in no case enter into the kingdom of heaven. [Kingdom of
Heaven is here, you have to be righteous in order to enter into
it.]*   —MATTHEW 5:20

*And as ye go, preach, saying, <u>The kingdom of heaven is at
hand.</u> [approaching]*   —MATTHEW 10:7

*And from the days of John the Baptist until now the kingdom of
heaven suffereth violence, and the violent take it by force.
[past and present]*   —MATTHEW 11:12

145

And the disciples came, and said unto him, Why speakest thou unto them in parables? [11]He answered and said unto them, <u>Because it is given unto you to know the mysteries of the kingdom of heaven,</u> but to them it is not given. [12]For whosoever hath, to him shall be given, and he shall have more abundance: but whosoever hath not, from him shall be taken away even that he hath. [know the mysteries of the kingdom now]   *—MATTHEW 13:10-12*

But woe unto you, scribes and Pharisees, hypocrites! for ye shut up the kingdom of heaven against men: for ye neither go in yourselves, neither suffer ye them that are entering to go in. [here now, people entering or being held back from entering it now]   *—MATTHEW 23:13*

The Elect are Operating in Heaven

Matthew 24 and Mark 13 both record an amazing future event. When the trumpet sounds, angels will be sent to gather the elect from one end of heaven to the other. Just a few verses earlier, it says that Satan would try to deceive the elect. Those who have already left their physical bodies are no longer subject to the deception of the enemy, so this passage has to mean those who are still in their physical bodies. In other words, God expects His children to be about His business wherever that takes them. He expects them to be busy on Kingdom business in heaven and on earth.

And except those days should be shortened, <u>there should no flesh be saved: but for the elect's sake</u> those days shall be shortened. [31]And he shall send his angels with a great sound of a trumpet, and <u>they shall gather together his elect from the four winds, from one end of heaven to the other.</u>   *— MATTHEW 24:22, 31*

[22]For false Christs and false prophets shall rise, and shall shew signs and wonders, <u>to seduce, if it were possible, even the elect.</u> ... And then shall he send his angels, and shall gather <u>together his elect from the four winds, from the uttermost part of the earth to the uttermost part of heaven.</u>   *—MARK 13:22, 27*

Where Do We Dwell?

The spirit realm is real, and we are spirit beings. The scriptures demonstrate that no matter where we find ourselves, whether in our earthly body or not, we can and should be walking with the Lord.

The real question becomes not who you encounter in your spiritual walk, but where are you dwelling? You may currently be clothed with an earthly body, but God wants us sitting on heavenly seats conducting the business of His Kingdom every day. Scripture says we are to have our conversation in heaven.

All of this is only possible if we are operating in God-given discernment. We can only be effective in His Kingdom if we can truly discern both good and evil.

And hath raised us up together, and made us sit together in heavenly places in Christ Jesus:
—EPHESIANS 2:6

For our conversation is in heaven; from whence also we look for the Saviour, the Lord Jesus Christ:
—PHILIPPIANS 3:20

Jesus said we are to dwell with Him, to abide in Him. We know He is in heavenly places and that is where He so often welcomes us in our times of intercession. He wants us to walk with Him in the spirit.

Abide in me, and I in you. As the branch cannot bear fruit of itself, except it abide in the vine; no more can ye, except ye abide in me. ⁵I am the vine, ye are the branches: He that abideth in me, and I in him, the same bringeth forth much fruit: for without me ye can do nothing.
—JOHN 15:4-5

Responding To an Encounter

By now you should know the answer to every spiritual experience. The answer is always, PRAY. Allow God to direct your path and open the eyes of your understanding to discern good and evil. Embrace good, flee evil. At all times, seek the mind of Christ, seek the timing of the Lord and humbly lay aside your own desires, fears and plans.

Remember, God has a very special and important purpose for your life. Allow Him to fulfill His plan for you.

Be blessed, dear ones, may He who lives in eternity call you often to walk with Him there.

.

Look around and you will see prolific evidence that the spirit realm is invading the natural realm. It has always been there, but with the time growing short, the frequency and intensity of the interactions between the two is increasing exponentially. The Lord has always prepared His people for what is ahead. In order to accomplish God's purposes for building His Kingdom and in order to meet and defeat our enemy head on, we must operate in discernment.

Remember our enemy is the Father of Lies; he is the master of deception. Our souls and our minds, our emotions and our instincts are all easily fooled by his tricks. Only through the Holy Spirit's guidance, His promptings and learning to walk in the ways of God can we hope to remain undeceived. God has given us the gift of discernment exactly for this purpose.

> *But the natural man receiveth not the things of the Spirit of God: for they are foolishness unto him: neither can he know them, because they are spiritually **discerned**.*
> *—1 CORINTHIANS 2:14*

Discernment must be developed, must be exercised or it quickly deteriorates into mere suspicion and deduction. God is calling for His saints to partner with His angels to arise and take dominion of this earth. The heavens are being opened as we intercede on the Father's behalf. The very land that we stand on is crying out for the sons of God to rise up and take this planet. Saints are being summoned by the Lord to stand against the onslaught of the enemy.

Discernment does not just perceive things of the spirit realm; it perceives them and, allowing the Holy Spirit to open our understanding, knows what is of God and what is not.

But strong meat belongeth to them that are of full age, even those who by reason of use have their senses exercised to ***discern*** *both good and evil.*

—HEBREWS 5:14

Our prayer for you is that you will indeed learn to tell the difference between holy and profane; that you will know the timing of God and cooperate with Him in His plan and strategy for every situation. It is not easy to do, yet it is the key to both protecting yourself and defeating our enemy.

For the word of God is quick, and powerful, and sharper than any twoedged sword, piercing even to the dividing asunder of soul and spirit, and of the joints and marrow, and is a ***discerner*** *of the thoughts and intents of the heart.*

—HEBREWS 4:12

God's Word both teaches us to discern and is itself a discerner. Rely on the whole counsel of God, do not be limited by what you suppose or are told by others. Study to show yourself approved by God; continue working in His Kingdom and doing His will.

We bless you in Jesus' Holy name. Amen.

Recommendations

The following is a list of books and teaching topics in a suggested order of reading by topic. They are available from www.messengersofhiskingdom.com or www.pneumatikos.com.

Entering God's Kingdom
- His Kingdom Come
- Divers Tongues, Languages of the Saints
- *Proskuneo*
- Incense
- Sprinkling of the Blood
- Firstfruits
- Discerning the Kingdom of God

God's Thoughts and Ways
- Five-Fold Manual of Interpretation
- Seers Catalog, Knowing the Ways of God
- Manual of the Seven Spirits
- The Timing of God
- No New Thing
- Dreams and Visions
- God is Light
- Right Hand and Left Hand
- Selah
- The Galal Factor

Spiritual Authority and Warfare
- The Saints, Awaken the Mighty Men
- *Pneumatikos*, Preparing for War
- Princes
- Hierarchy
- Overcoming the Spirit of Infirmity
- Fighting the Good Fight

- Seers Catalog II, Discerning the Signs of Conquest
- The Olive Tree and the Anointing
- Seven Thunders Revealed
- Fire of God
- Breath of God
- The Day of the Lord of Hosts

Heavenly Realms
- Ministering with Angels
- Heaven
- Angels of Deception
- Gabriel
- Michael
- Ministering from our Heavenly Seats

Saints in Training Courses
- The Saint's Heart
- Purpose and Prayer Life
- Intercession
- His Kingdom Come: The Saints
- Divers Tongues
- Discernment
- Discerning Your Territory
- Ministering With Angels

About the Authors

The Father sent Paul and Joy Harrison out in 2007 after serving for 20 years as Associate Pastors for The Father's Church in Dallas, Texas. Birthing "Messengers of His Kingdom", an evangelistic teaching ministry called to bring the message of the saints to believers everywhere.

It all began in 1996 when God put a hunger for more into the Senior Pastor of The Father's Church, Ron Crawford and then dramatically and visibly shook the church body awake with a miraculous demonstration of His power in the life of Associate Pastor Paul David Harrison.

Originally a traditional Pentecostal church born out of the miracle revivals of the 1930's, it relocated to a prestigious neighborhood, grew into a "popular" church. By the 1990's, the once spiritually active church settled into a well-oiled, comfortable place of great tradition. That is - until God came down. He began touching lives all over the church; people repented of cherished sins and members came to pray daily. The gift of divers tongues was released and the calling to intimate commune with Father God was loud and clear. Intercession and worship became the message and mandate of the church. Those who preferred the safety of tradition and upset by the changes, moved on to other congregations.

The Lord turned all our focus onto Himself. For seven years, God simply taught us to pray and seek Him. He showed us many marvelous revelations, but more importantly He taught us how to abide with Him. In the seventh year, God began sending the pastors and members out in teams to share the message of the saints. God wants us to abide in Him and have an intimate relationship with His as our Father. God is giving gifts to the church, especially divers tongues, to enable intercession and worship. He is revealing His ways as He moves in His Seven Spirits and the five-fold offices He has established in the church. He is pouring out incredible revelations of His Kingdom, including the ongoing manifestation of His angels.

In 2002, God began bringing other congregations and individuals alongside The Father's Church; and soon The Saints Network was formed. Its mission is to equip and train the saints to step into the fullness of the Kingdom of God; it encourages a renewed passion for intimacy with the Lord and ongoing intercession for His purposes to be fulfilled.

Paul David Harrison comes from a long tradition of Baptist pastors. In the 1970's, his nuclear family came into the fullness of the Spirit and started attending The Father's Church where he met his wife Joy. Answering the call to ministry, he received his B.S. in Pastoral Ministry and Evangelism and began working in both children and youth ministry positions. In 1983, God sent Pastors Paul and Joy back to The Father's Church as Associate

Pastors. After a dramatic spiritual encounter in 1996, Pastor Paul's total focus became intercession. Eventually the Lord led him to develop Saints in Training (SIT) courses to prepare people to move in God's purposes and with God's power to truly see His Kingdom Come. Paul is the author of several books and numerous study manuals. He has ministered extensively in Africa, India, Europe and the United States, sharing with pastors and intercessors what God is revealing about His Kingdom and the saints. Although the Lord uses him in many different giftings, Paul simply calls himself a witness.

Joy Burns Harrison is a third generation Pentecostal believer. She served on the pastoral staff of the Father's Church as teacher and business administrator. Joy has a passion for studying the scriptures and her function within the church body is one of bringing context and clarity from God's Word around the many revelations being birthed in these days. Joy also designs leadership programs for an international technology firm. Joy travels internationally both in ministry and in business. She is the author of several books and the founding editor of Pneumatikos Publishing. Joy holds a B.S. in Accounting and a Master Trainer certification in leadership facilitation.

Made in the USA